# forgiveness
## *is* real

# BRUCE MAJOR

## A LIFE-CHANGING JOURNEY
## TO FORGIVENESS

# forgiveness
# *is* real

**AMBASSADOR INTERNATIONAL**
GREENVILLE, SOUTH CAROLINA & BELFAST, NORTHERN IRELAND

www.ambassador-international.com

# Forgiveness is Real

ISBN: 978-1-64960-500-9, paperback
eISBN: 978-1-64960-544-3

Cover Design by Hannah Linder Designs
Interior Typesetting by Dentelle Design
Edited by Martin Wiles

AMBASSADOR INTERNATIONAL
Emerald House
411 University Ridge, Suite B14
Greenville, SC 29601
United States
www.ambassador-international.com

AMBASSADOR BOOKS
The Mount
2 Woodstock Link
Belfast, BT6 8DD
Northern Ireland, United Kingdom
www.ambassadormedia.co.uk

The colophon is a trademark of Ambassador, a Christian publishing company.

# Dedication

*I dedicate this book to the Almighty Father God; His Son, the King of kings and Lord of lords; and the indwelling Holy Spirt on whom I rely for right relationship.*

*It's only because of these Three-in-one that I can tell the story of my rebirth into the family of God. This book is His story as told by me and lived through me, and therefore, God gets all the glory.*

*"Being confident of this, that he who began a good work in you will carry it on to completion until the day of Christ Jesus" (Phil. 1:6).*

# Contents

# Preface

I wrote this book in an attempt to obey God. As the psalmist wrote, "My mouth will tell of your righteous deeds, of your saving acts all day long—though I know not how to relate them all. I will come and proclaim your mighty acts, Sovereign LORD; I will proclaim your righteous deeds, yours alone" (Psalm 71:15-16).

The gospels testify of Jesus's life. We Christians know Jesus still lives and works in every believer's life. Through our testimony and encounter with Him, the Gospel of Jesus continues.

For quite some time, I felt God calling me to share the testimony of my life before Christ and how He changed me when I hit rock bottom. My life was quite a mess because of alcohol and drugs. This book covers some profound events during my time in the navy, my first marriage, my time in the army, and my present marriage. This story also testifies to what God did when I had nowhere else to turn but to Him.

I hope these words will encourage and give you hope. God is real and waits for us to turn to Him so that He can save us and help us get through whatever we face.

# Author's Note

I didn't know how to write a book, so I decided to start where I always do when trying to learn something new: Google.

After reading advice about how to be a writer, with many technical terms and ideas that made it seem quite complicated, I settled on the one instruction that simplified it: to be a writer, you must write. That's it. I disciplined myself to write my first manuscript, but when I finished, nothing happened. I saved it to my computer.

I knew God had prompted me to write my story, but I didn't know what to do with it. I didn't even want to show it to anyone, thinking it may not be good.

I started getting little hints about publishing it, thinking I could do this. An advertisement came across my screen on Facebook about Christian writers. Then, a friend mentioned something about publishing a book.

I felt as if I was finally getting the hint, and God was sending it. This was not the first time He'd dropped hints on me about things He wanted me to do.

I decided to make a bold move—to me, at least. I would get the ball rolling and try to get someone else involved. I posted to Facebook, asking if anyone knew of a Christian book publisher. I didn't expect any replies, but I immediately got two. One from a friend, which turned into an appointment with a publisher in a few days. After an encouraging interview with Samuel Lowry from Ambassador International, I received a contract the same day.

I hope and pray you enjoy my story.

# Acknowledgments

This book would never be possible if it were not for the following:

God—for working in me my entire life; for hearing and answering my prayers; for saving me, my wife, my marriage, and my soul. All glory goes to Him.

My beautiful wife, Milly—for your unending, unwavering love; for putting up with me and giving me more grace and mercy than I deserve; and for supporting me in the writing of this book.

Jim Vaughn—for being an amazing friend, a man of God, and my brother in Christ.

Daniel Moore—for also being an awesome friend, fellow Holy Smoker, and brother in Christ.

Jerry Hughes—for being patient with me, being willing to grow in friendship with me, being a strong sounding board when I needed one, and being generous.

Mark Davis and the men of Twelve Stones Bible study group—for allowing me to be myself, ask endless questions, express my views, and have such great listeners. I am blessed to call all of you my brothers in Christ.

Harold Robbins—for always being genuine with me, encouraging me, and helping me grow through our time with Restoration Bible study.

Henry Garrison—for always making me feel welcome whenever we meet and for your strong love for God.

Darlene Major—for having such a beautiful heart and always making me feel so important and for taking the time to understand me and my relationship with the Lord.

# Introduction

This book is an attempt to describe events that led me to become a born-again Christian. In addition, I pray that this book, my story, will encourage you to turn to God in times of difficulty. I pray that you come to understand that God can do amazing things, even change someone's character. Also, I pray that from reading this book, you can experience what it is to truly be forgiven, and how to forgive in a complete and permanent way.

It was only through God's mercy and grace that my salvation occurred. I offer an account of my years prior to becoming born again for two reasons. One is to perhaps show you that anyone, no matter how far they may be from the Lord, can be saved. Your past does not matter; God will meet you wherever you are. And second, I feel it's important to remember where I came from. It's a powerful reminder of how far I've come.

In no way am I attempting to glamorize or glorify my sins of the past. I am remembering just how much God has changed me in the present. These past events all lead up to the moment of salvation, my epiphany of truth, and my encounter with God that were centered around the one thing I love the most—my beautiful wife.

According to the American Psychological Association (APA), as discovered in a Google search, infidelity in the United States accounts for twenty to forty percent of divorces. Is it possible to overcome infidelity in a marriage? Is forgiveness possible? And if so, can the subject never be brought up again? My wife and I faced such a challenge. But we were not alone. God had a plan and worked it out to perfection.

I was a pothead from Rhode Island, but I got my act together during my enlistment in the United States Navy. I was deployed to the first Gulf War during Desert Storm while struggling through my first marriage with an abusive wife. After divorcing my first wife and having fun in the bar scene, I found a beautiful and exciting Latina woman from Puerto Rico. We were friends for almost a year before she agreed to marry me.

What happened after our marriage is beautiful, tragic, and glorious. As a result, we became new people who love each other more than we ever could with our own strength.

Paul says, "We know that in all things God works for the good of those who love him, who have been called according to his purpose" (Rom. 8:28).

# The Early Years

*"Start children off on the way they should go, and even when they are old they will not turn from it."*

Proverbs 22:6

I think every parent wants to train up a child in the way they should go. However, we all fall short. My parents were no exception, and neither am I. We are all broken from the beginning and are training up more broken people. The only hope we have is God's wisdom provided in His Word. If we don't search for His wisdom, we are left to our understanding, which places us in God's place.

My parents, Edward and Joan Major, gave birth to an incredible little boy in 1962—me. I might have scared them a bit because I had one particular flaw. Although I arrived with brown hair, blue eyes, and a beautiful smile, I also had a medical condition known as lymphangioma in my right hand, located on the palm side of my hand at the base of my index finger. This must have been quite an unwelcome surprise.

The doctors at Rhode Island Hospital chose Dr. Sexton to fix my compromised hand. He performed a skin graph, but it apparently didn't work. The doctors operated on my hand again when I was three years old. This time, they did so on the inside edge, between my middle finger and index finger. Again, the problem remained. Two more surgeries followed—one when I was six and the other when I was thirteen.

I had a good early childhood. I had a dad and mom; two older brothers, Kenny and Michael; and one older sister, Susan. We lived in a small, barn-red house with white trim at the end of McGregor Street in Providence, Rhode Island. The kitchen and living room were downstairs, and the three bedrooms were upstairs. My sister had her room, and we three brothers shared a room, which got quite crowded. We needed bunkbeds so we could have room to walk around.

We had a pool that my mom spent a lot of time cleaning. But it was worth it, since this was before air conditioning became common in homes. So sometimes, when it was hot at night and the window fan wasn't enough, Mom would wake us all up for a midnight dip. She knew we were sweating. Afterward, we got some of our best sleep.

We lived on a quiet street with friendly neighbors who took pride in their home's appearance. During this time, most people mowed their lawns with manual push mowers and trimmed the hedges and edges with yard scissors. Another common practice was hosing down the driveway and adjoining walkways. Our neighborhood was a nice place to live and play.

When I was in kindergarten, I met this beautiful, blonde-haired, blue-eyed girl and fell in love. Her name was Gracie Lu, and she took my breath away. I told my mother about her and that I wanted her to be my valentine for Valentine's Day, which also happened to be her birthday.

Mom convinced me to bring a present to her at her home. I discovered a shortcut through some neighbor's yards, which allowed me to get to her house quicker. I was scared to death, but she liked me so much that she agreed to be my valentine and my girlfriend.

One time, I took her fishing at Canada Pond. She said she would kiss me for every worm I found. I must have flipped over a hundred big rocks trying to rake in as many kisses as possible.

Our romance only lasted about a year. She left me for another boy in another neighborhood. The heartache hurt my self-esteem for a long time. I think it also caused me to have an aversion to blonde girls.

I had two main friends. Frank lived across the street. He was a year older than me. Sometimes, we played ball together, but at other times, he bullied me. Even after the bullying, being so bored, I would call him to play again. Years later, I ended the bullying after my mom let me learn Taekwondo.

Raymond was my other friend. He lived about three blocks down the back road from my house. He was a better friend. He always respected me, cared about me, and taught me a few things about life and church.

I lived in an Italian neighborhood, which meant everyone was Roman Catholic. Almost everyone went to church, but the only church available was the Catholic one. Many of my friends were altar boys, and everyone went to Sunday school. As part of the Catholic sacraments, we are baptized within the first year, followed by Confirmation and First Communion in subsequent years.

My father didn't go to church with us. I asked him why once, and he told me he was Baptist. He didn't like making a big deal out of the Catholic priest. The priest was no different than he and put his pants on the same way—one leg at a time. This attitude toward the priest stayed with me and is one reason I didn't embrace the Catholic church.

Mom dragged me to church every Sunday, making me put on my "Sunday best." Shoes, button-up shirt, tie, suit jacket—the whole uncomfortable nine yards. Then, she fought with me in the pews. "Get over here." "Put that down." "Stop fidgeting." "Get your finger out of your nose." "Stop playing with that."

I don't know what my mom expected me to get out of church. I was an adolescent boy with a lot of energy, who loved summer mornings. Caging me in tight clothes in a hot building with people wearing enough perfume to choke someone made me want to leave the church at the first chance I got. Besides, I had no idea what the priest said or why we had to get up and down and kneel constantly.

I did, however, love Sunday afternoons. The smells of the various foods being cooked were phenomenal—pasta, bread, sauce, and pastries. I ate at my house; then I'd visit my friends and hope to get invited to their meals, too.

Our neighbors all knew each other and took to heart the old saying, "It takes a village to raise a child." If I did anything wrong, my mother knew about it before I got home. But she didn't come out and tell me she knew. First, she asked if I had done whatever it was. This was a setup to see if I would tell the truth. After enough groundings and spankings, I learned about the secret spy network of neighbors. If I got caught by one of them, I knew I'd get a spanking before I even entered the house.

My mother gave me spankings with a black leather belt. I trembled the moment I saw it. It came across the back of my legs, but my tears began before I felt it as I thought about the pain it would deliver.

She used the belt because we often ignored the bedtime rule. We all had strict bedtimes. Mine was about 7:30 in the winter and around eight during the summer—a cruel time for a young boy.

Mom often called me inside while all my friends were still outside playing. Then, after a good cleaning, she sent me to bed ten minutes later. Imagine the torment as I heard my friends still playing, yet Mom expected me to lie down and sleep.

I often stuck my head out the window and watched them from my second-floor bedroom. Eventually, I would accidentally make a noise, and Mom would scream, "Get back into bed." A few minutes later, I would go back to the window again. Mom sensed I was up, yelled at me again, and I'd do my usual dash to the bed and fake sleep if I thought she was coming. If I repeated my actions, I was really in trouble.

I could hear the belt snap when mother brought the folded ends of the belt together and then quickly spread them apart. SNAP! By now, she was right over me, and I was terrified. I'd curl up in a ball, hide under the covers, and begin to cry. She would throw back the covers, grab my legs and stretch them out, then slap me across the back of my thighs with the leather belt while screaming, "STAY" (whack) "IN" (whack) "BED" (whack). After that, I'd cry myself to sleep.

My neighborhood was great for playing Manhunt, a game of hide-and-seek. We had two blocks of homes, backyards, bushes, trees, and such in which to hide. We called it Manhunt because that name sounded cooler than a baby hide-and-seek game. After all, we were big kids at eight years old.

Dinner—or supper, as some call it—took place promptly at five. We knew when it was time to come home because the five o'clock whistle blew. The whistle was a loud horn placed strategically throughout the city and residential areas to warn people of an incoming nuclear bomb attack and was tested daily at five p.m.

I should also mention the streetlights. Our parents expected us to be home before they came on. So if it was dark when we got home, we might as well come in with our pants halfway down, anticipating a good spanking.

Mom warned me to stay away from some of the kids in my neighborhood. Although I didn't understand at the time, she had a good reason (secret neighborhood spies). I didn't always listen, and that's when I got into the most trouble.

Peer pressure from those forbidden kids led to my addiction to cigarettes at the ripe age of eight. One of the kids would steal a cigarette from their parents, and we would all try it. By the time I turned ten, I could get my hands on my own pack of cigarettes using my allowance or "candy money."

Whenever I went home, I hid my cigarettes in a plastic bag and placed them under some leaves or at the base of a bush where I could find them later. When questioned, I would lie to my mother about smoking, but of course, she could smell the stench of the cigarettes on me, and so a spanking and a week's worth of grounding usually followed.

One week of grounding seemed like a lifetime at my age, especially when I needed a cigarette. After my release from home jail, I'd find my hidden stash and light up one as soon as I was out of sight.

Once, my mother was so exasperated with me that she begged my father do some disciplining. My father didn't care much about my smoking. After all, he smoked, but my mother pushed him to do something about my actions. I remember one time when he picked me up, brought me over to the bottom of the stairs, and yelled for me to get to my room, then proceeded to punt me like a football up the stairs. I never touched a step.

It wasn't all bad, though. We were a hockey family. My father played hockey; my brother Michael played hockey; I played hockey; and my sister was a hockey cheerleader.

I looked up to Michael. He was several years older than me. We watched him play for Hope High School. Hockey looked like fun. I liked the fast pace, the hockey skills, and definitely the hitting.

I started in the peewee league at the North Smithfield Youth Hockey Association. My father, who owned his own business, Major Auto Top, sponsored our team. My mother, who sat in the stands, laughed at how clumsy we were.

We couldn't skate, much less play hockey. We scrambled and fell over each other in a big pile while chasing after the puck. Then, someone would spit the puck out of the melee, and we'd start the chase again. Mom laughed so hard once that her false teeth flew out of her mouth and landed under the bleachers. But in our second season, we won the league championship.

Michael gave my parents a real scare one time. During a game, his hockey stick and anther player's hockey stick came together, causing the puck to hit my brother in the eye. My parents knew it was serious when they brought a medic over and then took him to the hospital. He needed two pins to hold his eye in place.

I have great memories of rushing home from school, throwing my books on the floor, grabbing my skates, and running to the pond for as much skating as possible before it got dark. At times, the whole neighborhood came out to skate. Sometimes, someone would shovel the snow to create a makeshift hockey area. Boots served as our goal.

Although this seemed like a good idea, we had a problem. If someone missed a pass or scored a goal, we had to spend the next ten minutes looking for the puck under the snow. Hundreds of them must be at the bottom of that pond right now.

Springtime meant baseball season. We had several fields near our house where kids our age could play, but playing posed a problem for me. I throw with my left hand, which means I must catch with my right hand—the hand with the lymphangioma tumor. If I caught a hard ball that hit my palm where the tumor was, my hand would swell faster than I could get the glove off. And the pain was excruciating, causing me to cry. Never, ever cry in front of your friends. That means teasing for the rest of your life.

I could, however, play softball. The softball was larger and didn't make it as deep into the glove. I was pretty good, too. My size intimidated the other players, and I had no problem hitting the slower pitches delivered in softball. I even played in a softball league—Hugo's Barber Shop—at the Boys Club in my neighborhood. Everyone got their hair cut at Hugo's—crew cut, of course.

The Boy's Club was a great place to hang out. They would allow public swimming a few times weekly in the indoor Olympic-sized pool. All the boys swam naked, and to this day, I'm not sure why we were not allowed to wear bathing suits. We also learned to shoot pool, play ball in the gym, and just hang out with kids from other neighborhoods.

Our family didn't have much money, but my dad worked hard and provided a decent living for us. His upholstery business was located on Eddie Dowling Highway (Route 146) in North Smithfield, Rhode Island.

I remember when my father would take me to work with him. He taught me how to take cars apart and put them back together. I removed and installed automobile seats, motorcycle seats, car rugs, headliners, door panels, convertible tops, and vinyl roofs.

I also learned to drive while working there. I wouldn't go far— just back the car in and out of the garage. But for a twelve-year-old boy, that was awesome. Sometimes, the seat wasn't even in the car because my dad was repairing it. This meant I had to sit on a milk crate, and if not that, then I'd need to sit on my bent foot. The bent-foot method also caused my first accident.

My father told me to get the old Rambler sitting outside and to bring it into the shop. There wasn't a seat, so I assumed the position on my foot. I had to back up a bit to clear the car in front of me. As I eased the car into reverse, just enough to clear, I hit the brakes too hard. The car rocked just enough to hit the huge ladder leaning against a house behind me. It crashed onto the car, denting the trunk.

I put the car in park, heart pounding, and went into the shop to tell my father. He already knew. My dad had heard the crash but, amazingly, remained calm. He asked if I was hurt. When I told him I wasn't, he told me to put the ladder back and bring the car inside.

I suppose this was like getting back on a horse after being thrown. I remember feeling pretty good that Dad still trusted me. He repaired the upholstery for free to make up for the damage.

As a boy, because I was raised Catholic, I was assigned a godfather, Ron Barrone. Ron was a good man. He and his wife, April, had one daughter, Lauren. Ron was also a Providence police officer—a motorcycle cop.

I liked Ron and spent many afternoons visiting his house. He taught me how to use power tools and do some landscaping. He also paid me to do landscaping in his yard. Later, in my early teens, without him knowing, I bought pot with the money he gave me. Satan has a way of manipulating situations and people.

Many people, events, and situations—both good and not-so-good—shape our lives. The ages between birth and three are critical years. However, the years after three are more significant in shaping one's character.

In many cases, at young ages, forgiveness is almost automatic. Even though my mother disciplined me harshly, I automatically forgave her. When the bully across the street picked on me, I forgave him quickly because I needed a friend. When Mom dragged me to church against my will, I didn't hold it against her. Even when my first girlfriend broke my heart and picked another guy over me, I still had loving feelings toward her.

But as we get older, forgiveness is more complicated. We seem to internalize the hurts, and they become a part of who we are. Our character incorporates unforgiveness. And if we dwell long enough on our wounds, they become a significant part of our identity as a victim.

God created us to forgive as He does. He made us in His image. Unfortunately, the more exposure we have to this world, the more difficult it is to behave as God created us to behave. Our character changes over time because of our experiences, changing us from His forgiving creation to a less forgiving one. But isn't it great that God's forgiving character never changes?

# Alcohol

*"Do not get drunk on wine, which leads to debauchery.*
*Instead, be filled with the Spirit."*

Ephesians 5:18

The Bible says a lot about alcohol. People abuse what is inherently not sinful. Wine and bread are not sinful in themselves, but drunkenness and gluttony are. When God's Word does not guide our lives, our sinful nature controls our behavior. A life controlled by our sinful nature will lead to one form or another of destruction.

Sin leads to death. For some, this could mean the end of respect for someone dishonest. For another, it might mean the death of a relationship with someone disloyal. And in some cases, it could mean literal death because someone has abused their body.

Without the self-control that comes from God, our sinful nature constantly looks for relief from this broken world—an escape from difficulties that come from living in God's fractured creation. Substance abuse is a common coping mechanism for that escape. But like every other coping mechanism, these addictions never provide the peace, which we seek. Through my intimate relationship with God, I have learned that only He can provide the peace I seek.

By the time I was ten, things had changed around my house. Then, slowly, they went wrong and got worse. My parents started going out at night to have fun. They were doing the Hully Gully and Electric Slide. I also started hearing words like "high ball," "scotch," and "screwdriver." I remember my parents talking about their nights out and then laughing while looking forward to doing it again.

My brother or sister babysat me while my parents partied. I liked this arrangement because they gave me a lot more freedom than my parents. I could come in later from playing and go to bed later.

Eventually, my parents didn't laugh about their going out anymore. In fact, they stopped going out altogether. But they still talked about drinking. Soon, they began arguing about it. Until then, I couldn't remember them arguing about much of anything.

Suddenly, my father wasn't around as much. My mother was always angry, and they fought anytime he was around. My dad was drunk, and my mother couldn't handle it anymore.

One time, with tears streaming down my face, I asked her, "Are you guys going to break up?" Both of them assured me that would never happen. I took their word for it.

Not long after that conversation, my father went away for a while. My mother told me he went to a halfway house to dry out. I had no idea what that meant, but I assumed he was going to a hospital to get better. I later found out that he had called Alcoholics Anonymous. Some guys went to his shop, got him drunk so he would cooperate, and took him to a rehab hospital.

When my dad got home from rehab, things looked as if they might get better. Darkness still hung over our home, but it appeared we were all moving in the right direction. No more fighting. Everything was sort of quiet.

After a year of my dad being sober, my mother told me they were getting a divorce. I remember running out of the house, down to the back street, and standing near some trees where I often played. I decided right then and there that I was not going to cry over this. I would go back into the house and take it like a man.

A day or two later, my mother moved to an apartment within walking distance. I remember coming home from school one day, and the house looked empty. The reality of it all shocked me.

My oldest brother, Kenny, had already married and moved out. Michael was attending college, and my sister moved in with my mother. Everyone had their lives all figured out but me.

Then, the obvious question came from Mom when she asked me with whom I wanted to live—her or my father. My heart told me there was no way I could leave my dad alone, especially since my mother had been the one who chose to leave, and my dad had only recently stopped drinking. I chose my dad. Someone needed to keep him sober, so I guess I was it.

Initially, it appeared that my parents had fun; but eventually, they became less responsible, dependable, and in control of themselves. To a young boy, it is a bit frightening to have the people you rely on make you feel as if they are no longer reliable. A child needs to feel as if their parents love each other. The connection between child and parents is so profound that they all feel what the other feels.

The Bible often refers to such a connection between God and us. Because He created us in His image, we are born with the ability to feel as He feels. We need healthy boundaries to protect us from repeating hurts. Sometimes, this means letting someone go so they can make their own mistakes and experience the consequences.

God can remove His hand of protection from us so that we experience the natural consequences of our actions. When we set boundaries to keep someone from hurting us, we don't stop loving them. Instead, we start loving ourselves a bit more.

My mother grew up with an alcoholic father and then married a man who became an alcoholic. She felt she needed some boundaries, so she divorced my father. That didn't mean she stopped loving him or that she did not forgive him. She forgave my father for her sake, not his.

God forgives our offenses and passes His peace to us through the sacrifice of His Son, Jesus. No addiction provides the peace we seek. Nor will unforgiveness. Only through the forgiving love of Jesus can we receive God's peace that surpasses all our understanding.

# Drugs

*"Fathers, do not exasperate your children; instead,*
*bring them up in the training and instruction of the Lord."*

Ephesians 6:4

Like most men—including Adam in the Garden of Eden while Eve conversed with the serpent—we tend to be nonconfrontational, and my father was no exception.

Paul tells fathers not to provoke their children to anger. Though I'm sure he never knew of this Scripture, my father took this to heart. But unfortunately, he occupied himself more with keeping himself sober than risking upsetting a relationship with me by being firm with discipline. This lack of firm guidance allowed me to go unchecked, and I indulged myself in some very risky behavior.

Paul intended his words to encourage respect and a certain amount of grace for our children, while guiding them firmly in the Lord's instructions and disciplining them with love when they stray. My father did the best he could with what he had. He also failed in some areas because of what he did not have: a clear understanding of God's Word. As long as I passed my subjects in school, he didn't worry about anything I did.

My father pursued a relationship with God only in areas relating to his sobriety. I doubt he ever read the Bible. Without knowing God's Word, he could not possibly guide me in the instructions of the Lord. So, he did the only thing he knew how to do—he became my friend, my buddy.

My father was the best buddy anyone could ask for. Since we were alone, I spent as much time as possible with my dad. I figured if I were with him, he wouldn't drink. At this time, I was thirteen. We stayed up late and watched *Saturday Night Live*, *The Honeymooners*, or whatever else was on television while we ate pints of coffee ice cream. I could go out with my friends, and he didn't ask any questions.

One day, I asked him for permission to smoke in front of him. His response was, "Are you going to smoke, anyway?" When I told him I was, he said, "Fine, I'd rather you not do it behind my back."

So, I bummed a Camel non-filtered cigarette from him. I could handle it. What he didn't know was that I had been smoking since I was eight.

I joined an over-fifty duck pin bowling league with my dad. They made an exception in my case because I was a decent bowler, I came with my dad, and I was mature for my age. I had a great time getting to know the guys every Friday night at Seekonk Bowling Lanes.

My dad and I experienced a lot of ups and downs. He lost his auto shop location on Route 146, during the divorce, so he had to move it to a place in North Providence. Business wasn't good, and he could no longer afford the mortgage on the house where we grew up; so, we lost that, too, and moved to an apartment my uncle Russel owned, which, by the way, was the home where my grandparents had grown up.

Because financial struggles strapped my father, he couldn't hold on to the shop in North Providence either. Consequently, we had to move the shop to a seedy part of Rhode Island—Central Falls. The locals there called it Sparkle City because of how all the broken beer bottle pieces lying around on the ground sparkled in the sun. There are bars on almost every corner.

I was in the eighth grade at Esek Hopkins Junior High when my parents divorced. Until then, I was a pretty good student with average grades. I had the honor of graduating in 1976—the year America celebrated her bicentennial. A lot changed that year.

My dad attended Alcoholics Anonymous meetings. My mother tried to get me to go to Ala-teen, but I didn't feel I needed to. I tried once, and it was just too lame for me. I liked going to AA meetings with my dad better. He had a meeting just about every night. In the beginning, I went to all of them. I fit right in. Everyone welcomed me as I sat around with them—smoking, drinking coffee, and listening to their stories. The smoke was so thick in those church basements that sometimes I could hardly see who was talking.

I heard some harrowing stories about what alcohol can do to people. I was proud of my dad when he got up and said, "Hi, my name is Ed, and I'm an alcoholic." I knew telling his story helped him. I was especially proud every time he received his pocket coin for each year he had been sober. We always celebrated with a cake.

I remember the slogans AA used to help recovering alcoholics deal with life's difficulties without picking up a drink—slogans like "Let Go and Let God," "Easy Does It," "First Things First," "But for the Grace of God," and "One Day at a Time," and the ever-popular Serenity Prayer: "God grant me the serenity to accept the things I cannot change, courage to change the things I can, and wisdom to know the difference."

Anytime struggles came, we would say, "Oh, well," and let it go—times like when we had to move the shop or change homes because we didn't have enough money. "Oh, well." It was our way of letting go and letting God, and it was better than my dad picking up a drink.

Occasionally, I visited my mom. She moved a few times but finally settled into a small apartment in North Providence. She was going to Providence College, which seemed weird. She was old. I was the kid. I was the one who should be going to school, not my mom. She was studying to become a lay minister. I had no idea what that entailed, but I knew it was a Catholic thing.

Usually, the only time I saw my mom was during holiday visits, except for the one time I visited because she had been "born again." Although she tried to explain the meaning, I didn't understand. She said she had found Jesus. I remember thinking, "Great. Now she's a Jesus freak."

From that day on, whenever I spent some time with her, all she talked about was Jesus. I'd roll my eyes, and she'd give me looks of disappointment, then stop talking about it. Her look kept me from visiting more often. What was the point? I'd visit; she'd talk about Jesus; I'd be confused and uninterested; and she would be disappointed in me.

I remember going into my dad's bedroom once to wake him for work and seeing him kneeling beside his bed. I asked him what he was doing and asked if he was okay.

He said, "Yes, son, I'm praying."

I asked him why he was praying. He said he prayed every morning and asked God to keep him away from a drink for that one day. I asked him about all the other days. He told me he prayed for one day at a time, and then at night, before he got into bed, he thanked God for that one day of sobriety.

Although I often hung out with my dad, I also needed friends my own age. So, I would get on my ten-speed bike and ride down to hang out on one of the street corners. In a nice, suburban neighborhood, lots of corners provided hang-out spots, but the corner of Langdon and Everson Street was the spot where everyone went. Since it was near Canada Pond, we could do stuff we didn't want the neighbors seeing—like smoking cigarettes—or we would hang out in the open where everyone could see us.

Things took quite a turn when a bunch of my friends and I went to the Boys Club to sign up for shop classes. At first, it was pretty cool. The instructor seemed nice and taught us how to make wood crafts.

The shop instructor's name was Mike C. One time, he invited my friends and me to see a haunted house. It didn't seem right to me, so I didn't go. I was the only one who refused the invite. When I saw my friends the next day, they all told me they got high smoking pot and had a blast. I didn't want anything to do with that.

Shortly after, they told me they were going out again with Mike and that I should go with them. After enough peer pressure, I finally went. That was the first time I smoked pot and got high. I remember telling myself it was only temporary and that I would stop later when I got older. But in the meantime, I became a huge pothead.

Everything became about getting high. When I got money— usually from working for my godfather Ron—I would stand on the street corner, waiting for a dealer to come by and sell me a dime bag.

Mike C. also introduced us to skiing. He took us to Pine Top, a small skiing hill in Rhode Island. Once my friends and I began skiing, we loved it and started making trips all over New England to Mount Stow, Mount Snow, Mount Killington, and others.

The ninth grade was great. I joined the hockey team at Hope High School in Providence, Rhode Island. My dad got up at 4:30 a.m. in the cold to have me at practice by 5:30. The green 1972 Buick Electra 225 took forever for the defrosters to clear the windshield from the half-inch thick sheet of ice on the window. With a Camel in one hand and an instant coffee in the other, he peered out of any small crack in the ice he could find and drove.

I'd get to practice—lugging my hockey gear—and be on the ice on time. My coach was a drunk, so practice seemed pointless sometimes. However, we all loved the game, so we went, anyway.

By now, I could skate like no one's business, backward and forward, but I couldn't handle the puck to save my life. I also loved hitting people and felt invincible with all my protective gear. But by the time I finished the tenth grade, pot and my street friends had become more important to me, so I stopped playing hockey.

I don't know if my father was being nonconfrontational or smart by not confronting me. Although he never accused me of anything, he did lecture me about booze and drugs by directing his lectures toward one of my friends. During those lectures, I would think how right he was. I didn't want to be a pothead forever. At the moment, however, I was just trying to fit in. I had plans for my future—the United States Navy.

During Dad's lectures, the navy always came up. This was his way of pointing out an alternative to how I was living. Doing so also gave me hope for the future.

When I turned sixteen and got my license, my dad sometimes let me take his Buick out for the night. The Buick was huge and could easily sit six of us. I'm sure my father worried until I came home, especially since we couldn't afford car insurance. A big accident would bankrupt him.

Eventually, I bought my own car—a 1970 Chevy Impala. I loved that car. I always had to work on it to keep it running, but I didn't care. It was mine, and it was freedom. I could take my car to the beach, skiing, school, or anywhere I wanted. And with my newfound freedom, I could also go clubbing. At only sixteen, I could get in and get served at most bars. I looked old enough and was with other kids who were old enough.

My favorite thing to do in the summertime was visiting the beach. Unfortunately, I did many things I shouldn't have done, too. My buddies and I visited the local pool and sports bars in the wintertime.

My whole word revolved around alcohol and drugs. But these things were never in my long-term plan for my life, and I managed to stay out of trouble.

We all have people we need to forgive. Sometimes, it's our parents or other family members. Sometimes, it's our friends. More importantly, we need to forgive ourselves. I made those bad choices. Perhaps, if I had dealt with my parent's divorce, I would have made better choices.

Had I chosen a different group of friends, I may have gone to college and gotten a degree. Maybe, I would have been more successful, owned a larger home, driven a nicer car, or worked at a more enjoyable job. But I was never in control. None of us are. My life turned out just as God had planned. God needed me to be right where I was, doing exactly what He knew I would do, to bring me to Himself when the time was right. I did ask Him to forgive my sins, and He reminds me that He is in control and has a purpose for me. That purpose includes forgiving myself or anyone else.

My father may have been more of a buddy than a father. He may also have been nonconfrontational regarding my behavior, but God watched over him and me, working it all together for good in His plan.

I watched my father turn his life over to God when he prayed to stay sober. I also watched my father humble himself when he testified in AA meetings. He took responsibility for his addiction, and I learned how to take things "one day at a time," how to "let go and let God," and how to "accept the things I cannot change."

My father died in May of 2009 after thirty-five years of sobriety. He never put a drop of alcohol to his lips again. My dad beat alcoholism by God's grace.

# The Navy

*"For everything in the world—the lust of the flesh,*
*the lust of the eyes, and the pride of life—*
*comes not from the Father but from the world."*

1 John 2:16

As I grew during my time in navy boot camp, God worked to change my desire for drugs—something at the time I fully intended to continue. However, in place of that desire, I developed a level of pride I did not have before. The navy trained me to accomplish things I didn't know I could do. As a result, I became more aware of myself and my abilities.

With this newfound pride in myself came a fleshly lust—for what I could do and whom I wanted. I had graduated from Hope High School in Providence, Rhode Island. Both my parents attended, and seeing them together without fighting seemed a little weird. After graduation, I wanted to take the summer off to relax before joining the navy.

I remember one hot summer morning being awakened by Evelyn Champagne King singing her hit song "Shame." Because it was so hot, the windows in the apartment my dad and I lived in were open, and the music from the speakers was so loud, it seemed as if it was right in the room with me.

I saw my buddy, Stan the Man, in his Chevy Impala outside. I immediately got out of bed, got in his car, and headed for the beach for a day of summer fun. Stanley and I had a deeper bond than I did with any of my other friends. I spent most of that summer with Stanley—that is, until she came along.

One day, I saw a girl walking by my kitchen window. She must have just moved in. She had long, black hair and looked great. After a week or two of seeing her walk by, I decided to find out who she was. The next time she passed by, I spoke to her. Her name was Sharon, and she went back and forth in front of my house because she was interested in me. I was excited since, until then, I hadn't had many girlfriends. I didn't think of myself as good-looking because I was skinny and had acne all over my face that I tried to hide with acne cream.

The one catch was that she was thirteen, and I was eighteen. My friends didn't take to her very well. Actually, no one did. My father feared I would get into trouble dating an underage girl. Her parents, however, accepted me with open arms. I spent a great deal of time at her house, which didn't leave much time for me to hang out with my other friends.

In October of 1980, I was destined for the Naval Training Center in Great Lakes, Illinois, but not before my brothers and sister threw a big going away party for me. They invited everyone I knew. Around fifty people packed into the tiny apartment where my dad and I lived. I partied all night with drugs, alcohol, and girls.

Because of the lymphangioma in my hand, I needed a waiver from the navy to join. My father made some calls, wrote a letter or two, and made it happen. I'm sure he probably did some begging to God, too, thinking that the military might be the only thing that would straighten out his son. And it did.

After boot camp, I did just what I had planned. I put on my dress blues, got in my car, and headed straight to Stanley's house. He was glad to see me. He kept smiling at me, excusing himself, coming back into the room, and smiling again. Before I knew it, one friend after another walked in. I didn't realize it, but Stanley was throwing me a welcome home party, and it was growing by the minute.

The party started with just a little alcohol, but after smoking my first joint since returning home, everything seemed to change instantly. I became withdrawn and paranoid. I didn't want anyone around me, and I was desperate to be alone. Smoking pot wasn't fun anymore. I got scared and embarrassed and left the party. I think I offended some people by leaving, but I couldn't help it.

I had dried out from alcohol and drugs during the eight weeks of boot camp. The navy had kept me so busy that I didn't even notice what was happening to me. After the party, I swore I would never smoke pot again.

The navy stationed me at Navy Air Station Oceana in Virginia Beach, Virginia. My official squadron—an A-6 Intruder squadron, VA-176 Thunderbolts—was on a cruise in the Indian Ocean. I had to wait for them to return before I could join them. Meanwhile, I was temporarily attached to another A-6 squadron, VA-85. During this short time, I washed planes. Also, during this time, I forgot my pledge never to use drugs again.

I made the mistake of using marijuana in my barracks. Afterward, I doused the place with an air freshener. Doing this signaled to the SPs (Shore Patrol) when they patrolled the halls that I was up to something.

I heard a knock and opened the door, and there they stood.

"What locker is yours?" they asked.

I pointed, and they went in.

As a sailor, a person is government property, so the patrol doesn't need a search warrant. They found my bag of pot, handcuffed me, and took me to the brig. A day or two later, I was brought before the Captain's Mast, where I faced the captain of VA-85.

"What do you have to say for yourself?" he asked.

"Look at my record. I have always done my best for the navy; and even after this, I will continue to do my best," I answered.

He looked at me and said, "Thirty days in correctional custody."

I left the room with my hands cuffed in front of me and with chains from my handcuffs to my leg irons—all the while carrying my sixty-pound duffle bag that dangled from my fingers.

A bus took me to the Correctional Custody Unit near Newport News, Virginia. I spent the next fifteen days shining my shoes and being harassed by petty officers with big egos. They released me early because my official squadron, VA-176, had returned from their cruise and they wanted me out.

VA-176 trained me to be a plane captain. That sounds impressive—and it was for a young man—but it just meant I inspected the aircraft before and after every flight. Ten other plane captains and I were also responsible for moving aircraft, tying down the aircraft with heavy chains we carried on our shoulders, riding in the cockpit when we towed the plane, fueling the aircraft, and operating the ground equipment needed to launch the airplane.

During this period, while on a cruise aboard the aircraft carrier *U.S.S. Independence* (CV-62) in the Mediterranean Sea, I smoked my last joint.

When my friend offered it to me, I asked, "Where on this ship are we going to smoke that and not get busted?"

"Follow me," he said.

I followed him to the flight deck and down to a catwalk where no one could see us. So, there we were, sitting on the catwalk under the cannon deck of the *U.S.S. Independence* on the Mediterranean Sea, and I smoked my final joint.

I studied hard and eventually became an AMH (Aviational Hydraulics Mechanic) for the A-6 Intruder. Later, I became a troubleshooter in my field, which meant I went out on the flight line (land) or flight deck (carrier at sea) and troubleshot any problems that might arise just before the aircraft departed.

I remember one night at sea, standing on the flight deck. All was quiet; the sky was dark but clear; and the stars reached down to the horizon in every direction. I thought, *Wow, I've come a long way from the punk I was in Rhode Island.*

Suddenly, the sky lit up, and a shooting star zoomed over my head. Then, as the seawater sprayed over the bow and went down into the wave, I stood there, remembering what my father once told me about the navy.

Being a Navy veteran who served on the aircraft carrier *U.S.S. Roosevelt* during the Korean War, he said, "Son, sometimes, you're gonna wish you never joined the navy, but at other times, you're gonna be real proud you did."

This was one of those latter times.

Although my time on the flight deck was exhilarating, I had my most profound experience below deck in my bunk, which was directly beneath the flight deck. But I wouldn't realize just how profound this was until much later.

During some downtime, I decided to write to my mother. I rarely wrote to anyone other than an occasional letter to my girlfriend, Sharon. I never wrote to my mother with whom I had almost nothing in common. So, I decided to write her a poem and, of all things, about God.

I knew nothing about God, other than He may or may not exist. None of these things seemed to matter. I just wrote. I mailed it and never gave it another thought. I would not realize the personal profoundness of this poem for twenty-eight years.

On the next mail call, I received a letter from my mother. She told me that she loved the poem, so much that she had it published in her local church bulletin. This was a huge surprise, since I didn't think it was a good poem or even remember what it said. But if my mom loved it, that's all that mattered.

I wrote Sharon occasionally, but while I had land duty at Oceana, I spent rolls of quarters almost every night talking to her on the phone. I used a phone booth at the local club on base and spoke to her for hours.

If I had the time on paydays, I flew to Rhode Island to be with her, even if it was only for a day or two. She had captured my heart. Sharon was the main reason I didn't stay in the navy. I was away too long, and I wanted a family. I had also seen families break up during my time in the navy. No one wanted to get a "Dear John" letter.

During my visits home with Sharon, my suspicions of her cheating always got the better of me. Even though she calmed me down, reassured me, and convinced me she was not, I often saw her running after other men.

After three years of active duty, I finished my full-time commitment to the U.S. Navy. I thought that maybe things would improve between Sharon and me. I was wrong. She didn't change at all.

One night after hanging out with her, I didn't go home but staked out her house to see if she was seeing someone behind my back. As I waited, a cop knocked on my window. Someone had reported a strange person in the parking lot. I told him why I was there.

"She's a ball-and-chain. Break away now," he said.

The next day, I broke up with Sharon. I had a lot of which to be proud. I was a naval aviation hydraulics mechanic aboard one of the most powerful warships in the world. I had gone places and seen things of which my buddies back home could only dream. I had an enormous responsibility and was good at what I did. But I had a lot of work to do in relationships.

I realized jealousy is dangerous. Jealousy grows from a lack of trust and a constant state of fear. Of course, being jealous gets explosive. I'm grateful God used someone to point this out to me before I hurt someone. Fortunately, the only hurt that came from my jealousy was my pride.

Scratch the surface of any sin, and we will unearth pride. Pride is what got the best of Satan. Because of Satan's pride, he wanted to be God, and look where that got him. Pride is a massive barrier between us and forgiveness. As long as we pick at the wound that our pride has suffered, we won't forgive—nor will we heal from the wound.

People say forgiveness is for us, not the offender. And that's true. But we must understand that the hurt is mostly pride. We've been slighted, abused, or violated in some way; and even after the offense has ended, pride keeps us clinging to the hurt. However, we can forgive once we realize what is holding us back. Imagine the amount of pride Jesus, the Creator of the universe, had to swallow on the cross for our sake.

# My First Wife

*"Better to live on a corner of the roof than share a house with a quarrelsome wife . . . Better to live in a desert than with a quarrelsome and nagging wife."*

Proverbs 21:9, 19

The whole idea of marriage has become such a complicated and stressful issue recently. People have little guidance or standards in this area and feel they need to figure it out for themselves.

I was no exception. I married because it seemed logical at the time. Though marriage is a logical step in the progression of a relationship, there are also far more important reasons to marry as well. To succeed in marriage, we must take the first step by asking God what He has planned for us. The rest will work itself out if we keep God at the center.

Though I had completed my active-duty time in the navy, I still had reserve time to finish. So the navy assigned me to VP-92 Minutemen at NAS South Weymouth in Massachusetts. I worked on the airframe of two anti-submarine patrol aircraft, the *SP-2H* and the *P-3 Orion*, while completing my commitment to the U.S. Navy Reserve.

During high school, I had taken a mechanical drawing class that taught me how to draw detailed blueprints for machine parts. I loved this class and can remember thinking I would love to do this for a living someday. Now that I was home from the service, I got my chance.

I enrolled at Hall Institute of Technology in Pawtucket, Rhode Island, and learned how to make blueprint drawings for machines and machine parts on a drafting board using precise drawing instruments. I learned about drafting techniques and how to make parts to precise tolerances. This was an art form. With multiple line weights, exact measurements on paper, and precision lettering, drafting required a substantial number of artistic abilities wrapped up in a restrictive set of standards and rules. I was good at it, and with experience, I knew I could make a lucrative living.

During my time at Hall Institute, I lived with my father and made do with what money the navy reserve provided. I frequented my favorite local pub, McCormick's Pub, and eventually became a short-order cook in their kitchen. This allowed me time to meet many girls.

I first met Carrol at McCormick's. When I saw her for the first time, she was sitting in a booth, crying. I asked her what was wrong, and after talking for a while, she confessed she was pregnant. She also told me the father refused to acknowledge the baby, and that's why she was crying.

Carrol and I became friends. We hung out at the bar and talked. I helped her with rides and getting around because even at twenty years old, she did not have a license. She lived at home, and I got to know her mother, too. I knew her brother from high school, so

I was familiar with the family, but now I got to know them more intimately.

On May 29, 1986, I was on a charter boat with a bunch of my buddies, fishing for blues in Narragansett Bay. I caught about twenty—the best fishing day I had ever had. At the end of the day, we went to McCormick's to brag about our catch. When I got there, I learned from the bartender that Carrol had gone into labor and had a baby girl. I was excited to learn that the baby was born on my birthday. Not long after that, I asked Carrol to marry me.

I fell in love with Baby Agnes and the role of being a daddy, even though she wasn't my blood child. Carrol and I were already dating, so I assumed this was the right thing to do. Even now, when someone asks why I married her, I give a quote from Mr. Spark's father on Star Trek: "It seemed like the logical thing to do at the time."

As soon as we got home from our honeymoon, we discovered Carrol was pregnant again. I was in the delivery room this time when Candice entered the world. She was a big baby at ten pounds, two ounces and was the most precious thing I had ever seen.

By then, I had a good job as a draftsman at Hub Folding Box Company in Mansfield, Massachusetts. Our family was growing too large to stay with Carrol's mother, so we got an apartment of our own on Charles Street in Providence.

Shortly after moving in, Carrol began to change. I don't know what she was going through, but nothing I did pleased her. She complained about everything. I cleaned the house, fed the babies, got up in the middle of the night to care for the babies, made dinner for us, worked, did the dishes, and vacuumed the floors. My heart was all in. The only thing I got in return was nagging and complaining. Either I didn't do it right, was no good, or didn't do enough. We began fighting all the time.

My father taught me to cherish women, and I was doing everything I could to maintain respect for my wife. My father also taught me never to hit a woman. One night at supper, she started in on me again. I got so angry that I threw my pizza at the wall and shot out of there as fast as possible before I lost my cool and did something I would regret.

Carrol tried to isolate the children and me from my immediate family as well. We got invites to my nieces' and nephews' birthday parties, holiday get-togethers, and other special events, but Carrol would never accept. She would either not tell me about the invitations or would continuously complain about having to go. On the extremely rare occasion that we did go, she would sit by herself, making these occasions difficult for me and my whole family.

One time, when we got home after an event, she said my mother and sister-in-law told her they didn't like her and to never return and to stay away from their kids. I was dumbfounded. I could not believe my family would say such things or be so hurtful. After about the third time that Carrol had made these accusations, I brought my mother over for a face-to-face talk, hoping to clear the air. I cried a ton of tears, and we stopped attending family functions. Carrol brought out the worst in me.

Then, I got a new job as a draftsman at a chemical plant in Bristol, Rhode Island. While there, I met a guy who told me about the Rhode Island Army National Guard and the extra money he made one weekend per month and two weeks per year during summer training.

He also told me about a unit located in Pawtucket, Rhode Island. He encouraged me to check it out.

I had completed my time in the navy and had no further obligations to the military. However, this extra money and time away from Carrol intrigued me. I went to the 115 Military Police Company in Pawtucket to check it out. It was the Friday evening of a drill weekend, and busy soldiers crowded the place. I found out from the commander that I could sign up on a one-year trial basis. If I didn't like it, I could get out. I would keep my rank of E-4 (Petty Officer Third Class in the navy, Specialist in the army), and after the year, if I signed on for another six years, I could get an enlistment bonus.

In 1987, I signed up. After reporting to drills for one year and training for two weeks during the summer, I realized I liked playing with guns, driving jeeps, and camping out. So, after the year, I signed up for six more years and got the bonus. I enjoyed my time with my army buddies and the break it gave from constantly fighting with Carrol. The extra money also helped.

After a few job changes, I landed an excellent job at Taco Pumps in Cranston, Rhode Island. I made a great friendship with one of my co-workers. Carl was a bodybuilder and taught me about strength training at the gym. My kids called him Uncle Lumpy because of his muscles.

In August 1990, Saddam Hussein invaded Kuwait. Shortly after, America went to war to liberate Kuwait, and the U.S. Army selected the 115 MP Co. to prepare for deployment. So, we were prepared strategically and militarily, but it was different inside our hearts.

Knowing we were going to war was a serious thing. The military had trained me to believe my primary mission was to win in any situation I faced. And that presented a moral dilemma for me. I felt the optimal way to win a war was to shoot and kill the enemy without them shooting and killing me. Of course, the best way to do that would be to sneak up on the enemy and kill them first. But what would God think of me? Or worse, what if I was good at it and liked it? Suddenly, war became a really big concern—not for fear of dying, but for fear of living. I needed to talk to someone, so, of all people, I spoke to my mother.

My mother suggested I talk to Father Paul, a priest she knew well. He was the perfect man to talk to. During the Vietnam War, he was the guy on the medivac helicopters who picked and chose which wounded soldiers would get medical attention and which would not. I respected him because of his experience. He told me what I needed to hear.

"God gave you the instinct to defend yourself, and you know that if you don't, the enemy will kill you first."

That sounded obvious and simple, but I needed to hear it from someone who knew God better than I did.

We trained in the snow at Fort Devens, Massachusetts, pretending it was desert sand. Until now, our training had been a mix of garrison duty (police duties on a military base) and some light combat training. Now, it was all combat.

Anytime we were near a television, we heard Saddam Hussein's rhetoric. He made biological and chemical weapons a genuine concern for us and everyone. Finally, we boarded a plane at Westover Air Force Base in Massachusetts. Our unit was divided into several planes that carried our gear, equipment, and Hummer vehicles for the fourteen-hour flight to Dammam, Saudi Arabia.

When we settled into our new homes, we slept on army cots and made tables out of boxes of old MREs (meals ready to eat). We added a few personal items, like pictures and flags, to the walls. I kept a picture of my daughters and my wedding day on my wall.

On February 24, 1991, we were informed that the ground war had begun. This put many of us on a heightened state. But unfortunately, we did not receive daily reports from CNN or other news outlets like our fellow Americans did.

On a Monday, just before my evening shift, I suddenly heard and felt the ground shake from a loud BOOM! After dismissing several possible causes, I assumed our base might be under attack.

Accepting this possibility, I experienced something I had never before experienced. I got furious, but not in a common way. My anger became extremely intense; my senses became incredibly heightened; and my mind became sharp and calculating. As I quickly donned my personal protective gear (used to protect us from chemical or biological attacks), all I could think about was how dare someone try to take me away from my baby girl.

Once I stepped outside with my M-16 locked and loaded, I realized that we were not under attack. I quickly came down from my adrenaline rush when I bumped into my first sergeant, who told me to stand down. It turned out that a SCUD missel had landed nearby, and we needed to respond with military police support.

After returning to our regular patrolling duties and at my first opportunity, I stopped at a phone booth, called Carrol, and told her what had happened. I was sure to mention that all of the 115th soldiers were fine, and no one got hurt. I had no idea how important that call was to wives back home. Carrol later called the wives' support group and told them we were all okay. When I returned home, I received many hugs and thank you's from women I had never seen before.

Although I didn't purposely go to war to live in the desert as described in Proverbs 21:19, life was complicated—but simpler than living with Carrol. I tried so many times to forgive Carrol for her abuses. I wanted to save our marriage, primarily because of the kids, but it was too difficult to stay and subject myself to her constant torment.

Forgiveness was a continuous exercise while I lived with Carrol. After I forgave, she would offend me again. It was her norm. I assumed her childhood had conditioned her for this kind of rollercoaster. But I was getting nauseous and needed to get off. My sense of loyalty and desire not to fail in my marriage gave me the will to continue with her after returning home from the war.

Sometimes, the line between tolerating something and forgiveness can blur. For example, after forgiving, I always felt as if I were getting a new start, but maybe I just endured her abuse.

# Divorce

*"'The man who hates and divorces his wife,' says the Lord, the God of Israel, 'does violence to the one he should protect,' says the Lord Almighty. So be on your guard, and do not be unfaithful."*

Malachi 2:16

God hates divorce. He also realizes we will make poor choices, especially if we don't consult Him first when choosing a mate. Therefore, God has made a way out through divorce, as He made a way out of our sinfulness through His Son, Jesus.

At the time of my divorce, I was not a follower of Jesus Christ but a follower of this world. So naturally, I looked to the world for a solution to my failed marriage. I filed for divorce.

When the time finally came for the 115 MP Co. to go home, there was no fanfare, no whooping and cheering, no pretty stewardesses waving flags like all the units had before us; we were just a bunch of tired soldiers. All the hype about troops coming home was long over. Those things didn't matter to me anymore. I was just glad to be going home. The Armed Forces radio announced that it was 128 degrees outside the day I left Saudi Arabia.

Upon arrival at Westover Airforce Base in Massachusetts, we were anxious to see who awaited us. An exciting reception of family members all gathered for our return. I was not disappointed when I saw my mother, Carrol, and my two girls, Candice and Agnes.

First, of course, we had to fall in line for a quick debriefing before we were dismissed, and we were all chomping at the bit, ready to explode into our loved one's arms. I couldn't have felt any greater feeling than when both girls ran up to me and put their arms around my neck. I scooped them into my arms to absorb all the love I could get. Carrol seemed happy but was also upset because she had to ride with my mother.

After a quick reunion, we returned to Rhode Island. The next day, we still had to report to duty to take care of equipment, get a more in-depth debriefing, and meet counselors. I remember one thing the counselor told us. After reminding us that our spouses had been getting along without us for the last seven months, he said if we had any inclination to leave our spouse, now was the time. They had already adjusted to life without us, and it would be less complicated if we got it over with. Up until now, the thought had never crossed my mind.

I returned to my regular job at Taco Pumps and my everyday life. My pay at Taco was high enough for me to buy a house. I could use my VA benefit, so I didn't need a large down payment. I bought a house on Wilson Street in the Oakland Beach area of Warwick, Rhode Island. It wasn't a great house. The bathroom was tiny; the bedrooms were small; my bedroom was a poorly made addition to the home; and the house felt damp all the time. But it was mine, and I loved the area near the ocean. I thought buying the house would improve my marriage. I was wrong.

I continued to do all the cleaning in and outside the house. I took care of the kids, ran all the errands, and worked my full-time job. None of it was enough. Carrol continued to abuse me verbally and emotionally.

Every day when I left work to go home, I'd stop to buy a beer for the ride, and I would have an imaginary fight with Carrol before I even got home. It got to a point that I knew she would start in on me as soon as I walked in the door, and I was defending myself before I even got there. Then, the abuse began when I walked in the door, and it didn't end until I fell asleep.

One day, while I was sitting on the couch trying to watch television, I heard Carrol scream for the girls to come downstairs. As they stood in front of their mother, she screamed at them, swore at them, and berated them for their lousy job cleaning something. She told them they were no good.

Then, Carrol took them upstairs. Something changed in me as soon as she was out of my sight. It was as if a light switch had turned on. I stood up, grabbed my coat, and left. I was done.

Not knowing where to go, I went to my brother Kenny's house. I told him everything, and he agreed to let me stay there until I could get my own place.

My mother had a lawyer friend who agreed to take my divorce case. My main goal at first was to establish visiting rights and a schedule. This was not as easy as it seemed.

We had court appearance after court appearance, trying to get a hearing before a judge. Carrol fired one lawyer after another, all of whom helped her pro bono. I paid for mine, and the bill was adding up. We also had to work out child support payments. That part gained a judge's ear right away, but my right to spend time with my daughter Candice took months.

When I finally got to visit with Candice, Carrol also made me take Agnes. The truth was that Agnes was a spy for Carrol. I don't believe Agnes even knew how her mother used her.

Eventually, my lawyer advised me only to take Candice, who was legally mine. He tried to protect me from frivolous or false accusations by Carrol, which could ruin my chances of seeing Candice. My lawyer had the foresight to set me up for drug and alcohol testing weekly before Carrol could accuse me of having either or both of those problems.

Sure enough, Carrol lied and said I had a drug and alcohol addiction. When we appeared before a judge about it, the judge decided I needed supervised visits by the family court. I would have to see my daughter at family court or have their representatives present if I saw her somewhere else. After just a few visits, the counselors knew Candice and I were getting a bad deal.

One difficult time comes to mind during these few years of family court struggles and disappointments. I hadn't seen Candice for months because Carrol denied me a visit, and the courts delayed my chance to be heard. But on this one time, it appeared as if I might get to see a judge. Then, Carrol fired her lawyer, and things remained the same.

After this huge disappointment, I visited my mother, broke down, and cried. I felt so defeated. For the first time I could ever remember, my mother comforted me by letting me lay my head on her lap as she ran her fingers through my hair. Up until now, she had never shown me such affection. She also did one other thing. She took a tiny slip of paper, wrote something on it, and told me to place it in my wallet. She didn't tell me what it said, and she told me not to read it until the next time I felt overwhelmed. I did as she told me.

The next disappointment came along quickly. We had another court appearance scheduled; Carrol had another lawyer, and it appeared something would finally get done. After waiting a few more weeks, the time came. We went to court, and her lawyer said she needed more time to read over and get familiar with the case. I thought the insanity would never end.

I remember going to work right after court, sitting at my desk, and crying my heart out. Then, I remembered the paper my mother had given me. I pulled out my wallet, found the paper tucked inside, opened it, and read it. All it said was, "Jesus." I reread it. After the third time, I felt at peace. The crying stopped; my mind cleared; and I didn't feel so overwhelmed anymore. I was amazed at how much peace I got from just saying, "Jesus."

I went through quite a few changes during these years. I left the Rhode Island National Guard. I told them it would be challenging to meet my commitment to the Guard because I visited with my daughter on the weekends. My captain understood and said he could put me on "Inactive Reserve" status for the remainder of my commitment.

Also, my job at Taco ended. I had a boss who insisted I enroll in college, and when I didn't, he laid me off. Then, I got a new job at Serec Corporation in Providence as a designer draftsman. By now, computers had taken over drafting.

During all of this, I moved out of my brother's house and rented an apartment. Tenement houses filled the north end of Providence. Stanley's family owned a six-tenement house, and one of them became available when I needed it. I got the first floor in the front, facing the street. Stanley and I were practically neighbors because he lived on the third floor above me.

This living arrangement gave Stanley and me a chance to get closer and relive our partying days. We loved going to the beach and hitting all the bars.

The first girl I began a relationship with after Carrol was just like her. Once I realized this was another Carrol, just in a different package, I ended it. I realized I would continue to attract the same kind of women unless I changed. So, I started going out of my way to find girls who were nothing like my ex. I discovered such women were not that difficult to find.

Growing up, I had never considered myself handsome, but I guess I aged well. Soon, I met Jane, who was unlike any of the other girls. We hit it off well, and I considered her my first real girlfriend after Carrol.

Jane was older than I and had an adult son in his twenties. They were from Texas, and her son was passing through Rhode Island on his way to Green Bay. Jane planned to go to Green Bay with him, then come back. She made plans for me to meet him, which was a big deal for me. I made a nice pasta dinner and ensured my apartment was clean, but I worried her son might not like me or that we were too close in age. I cared a lot for Jane, so I was deeply hurt when she never showed up and never called.

Like Jesus, we must forgive. If we want to be forgiven for not consulting God in our choices, not putting Him first, and not letting Him be our Lord, then we must forgive—even our ex-spouses.

After my marriage with Carrol ended, she kept abusing me by not letting my daughter have a healthy relationship with me. She also made false accusations against me.

But in the middle of this unfair and horrible custody battle—in which Satan meant me harm—God used it for good. I cried out to Jesus when I was at my lowest, and for the first time, I experienced the power of His name.

# Milly

*"A wife of noble character who can find? She is worth far more than rubies. Her husband has full confidence in her and lacks nothing of value. She brings him good, not harm, all the days of her life. She selects wool and flax and works with eager hands. She is like the merchant ships, bringing her food from afar."*

Proverbs 31:10-14

I have no doubt God brought Milly and me together. Neither of us knew God nor consulted God about each other, but knowing what I know now, God blessed us with each other. However, we would go through so much pain before we understood that. Our love was tested in so many ways.

One Friday night, Stanley and I went out for something to eat. Stanley told me about a sports pub I'd never heard of. At this time in my life, I was always game for checking out new places. The bartender was beautiful and had a smile that lit up the bar.

After eating, Stanley and I took our drinks and headed for the back of the bar to shoot a game of pool. When the bartender finished her daytime shift, she joined us. I found out that her name was Milly, she had a son named Xavier, and she was from Puerto Rico.

Milly and I hit it off immediately. I guess it became obvious to Stanley, so he suggested, where she could hear, that I ask Milly out on a date. Feeling cornered but confident, I asked her to accompany me to a pool parlor called Boston Billiards. I knew she liked to shoot pool—she even had her own two-piece, custom pool cue—and Boston Billiards was not a dive bar. She agreed.

Although I made it clear I wanted a romantic relationship with Milly, she made it clear that we were to be just friends. Milly quickly became the most unique friend I ever had. She would pick me up at my house after work, and we would drive around, talking and listening to Spanish music. She would sing the lyrics to the songs and interpret them for me. You can learn a lot about someone from their choice in music.

The Latino music that Milly translated to me was full of love, passion, and romance. I got to know her through this music and realized that although she was nine years younger than me, her maturity level was more remarkable than most women my age.

For some reason, Milly also talked a lot about her previous boyfriends. She had dated older men because it was safe. They treated her like gold, but she never got too attached in her heart, so leaving them was easy. She had a wall around her heart. The more time I spent with her, the more I wanted to spend with her. I could tell that she felt the same.

Milly lived with her mother, Nelly; her brother; and her sister. She also had a brother, who spent much of his time in and out of jail. Milly's family mainly spoke Spanish, so I usually had no idea what anyone was saying whenever I visited.

Nelly loved me from the start and treated me like a king. She always made sure I was comfortable. What English she did speak always included nice things about me, and she always put me at the head of the table and fed me first.

Milly and I became great friends and though I wanted more, she insisted I stay in the "friend zone"—that is, until Jane showed up. Jane was returning to Rhode Island for a few days and needed a place to stay. I assumed this wouldn't be a problem for Milly, since she said we were only friends. I was wrong.

Jane hadn't been at my house for a day when Milly first told her and then me that she needed to leave. When I saw how upset Milly was, I knew she felt more than a friendship toward me. While there, Jane wanted to give our relationship another try, but I refused. She had hurt me too much.

Milly set up our first real date as a romantic couple. In pure Milly fashion, she took me to a very classy place called Bovies in East Providence. It was a small, romantic bar and restaurant with white linen tables and great food. The main attraction was an all-brass band playing right up close in the same room. Here, we had our first kiss. I was so happy and grateful that our relationship moved beyond friendship and eventually marriage.

Just one thing made our relationship less than perfect. I smoked cigarettes and had since my father had permitted me to smoke at thirteen. Then one day, as Milly and I were leaving a bar, I decided to quit. I was in the most exciting relationship of my life and didn't want anything to get in the way. So, when we got to her house, I threw my cigarettes in the trash and quit cold turkey. I told her our relationship was perfect, and I didn't want any "butts" to come between us.

I turned to exercise to help me overcome my habit. I had a rickety, old workout bench and some weights in the basement of my apartment that would help me overcome the smoking and my divorce. I also refurbished my old ten-speed bicycle and rode it to work whenever I could and then again to see Milly after work. On weekends, I jogged.

Milly was my sole focus, and my love for her grew quickly. She was so beautiful, insightful, intelligent, and generous. Best of all, she loved me. No other being had ever shown me so much affection. I had had other girlfriends, but their level of affection was always reserved. Milly loved me for who I was.

At this point in my life, I discovered something about men I once thought only women experienced: a desire for a child. I had always assumed a woman's biological clock governed the human race. Not true. When a man finds the right woman, he, too, often has the same desire. Milly caused me to want a baby.

Now that we were a couple, we needed a place of our own. Moving into my place would have made her uncomfortable. It was *my* place. We couldn't move into her place because she lived with her mother. So, we found a home we could call "ours" in Johnston, Rhode Island, on the third floor of a three-tenement house.

I decided to surprise Milly one day with tickets to see one of her favorite singers, Robert Cray, a blues guitarist and singer. She was so excited. We sat near the stage. I looked at her and asked, "Isn't life easier with me?"

My heart sank when Milly said, "No."

I got so angry, I gave her all the money I had in my pocket and the keys to the car and left. I started the six-mile walk home angry, talking to myself the entire way. I couldn't believe she would say that. I was all in and thought she was, too. I had given her my whole heart.

When I finally got to the driveway, I noticed the car wasn't there. My fury became rage. How could she still be at the show enjoying a good time? She didn't even bother to come home or look for me.

Instead of going in the house, I walked to the store and bought a pack of cigarettes. I lit one up and then walked back to the house. She still wasn't there. As I sat there on the couch smoking, she finally came home. Then she came over, took the cigarette from my hand, crushed it, and said, "Not easier, but better." Then she kissed me.

My anger melted away, and the cigarettes went into the trash. Neither of us can remember how the proposal went, but we both agree Milly proposed to me.

Milly and I had a small wedding at my brother Michael's house. We invited only immediate family and some close friends. We enjoyed a one-night honeymoon at a quaint little bed and breakfast called The Painted Lady in Narragansett, Rhode Island. We were so much in love.

Later, Milly became a correctional officer at the Rhode Island Department of Corrections. I had applied for the job, too, thinking they would pick me because of my military service, but they selected Milly.

I was very proud of her. I helped her through her training in any way I could. Using my military boot camp experience, I ensured her shoes were shined, and her uniforms were perfect. I also helped her train to run the required two miles. As a result, Milly graduated fourth in her class of eighty.

But the thing I was most proud of was our loving relationship. Unfortunately, my pride in this area nearly caused our downfall. One day, Milly told me about a friend she had made at the prison. His name was John. One day, Milly had invited John to come to the house around five that evening so I could meet him. Unfortunately, we forgot and didn't get home until eight. He was still there, sitting in his car. This was my first warning. Who waits three hours at the house of someone they just met? Though I found it strange, I blew it off.

Visitation rights over Candice continued to be a problem. Carrol would deny me my right to see her just about every time. On the Wednesday before Thanksgiving Day in 1993, Milly and I had just left the courthouse, where the judge had finally awarded me some time with Candice. He said I could have her that night and Thanksgiving weekend. He also adjusted the child support.

Milly and I went to Carrol's house to get Candice. She wasn't home when we got there, so we waited. Thirty minutes later, Carrol arrived, riding in her neighbor's car with Candice. When they got out of the car, Carrol's first words were, "Where's my money?"

Carrol refused to let me take Candice until I paid her and then told Candice to run inside the house. As I approached my daughter, Carrol grabbed her by the hand and ran inside the house with her. I walked back to my car, feeling defeated.

My next visitation was scheduled for the following Thursday, and Milly thought it would be a good idea to have a police officer meet me at Carrol's house to enforce the court order. I agreed, and Milly and I waited in the car about five houses away until the officer arrived.

We drove to the house to meet him when we saw him pull up to the driveway. I got out of my car, handed him the court order, and explained the situation. He took the court order, read it, and told me to wait in the car. He would get Candice.

When the officer returned, he didn't have Candice. He asked me to step out of the car, cuffed me, and read me my rights. Then he explained that Carrol had filed a complaint saying that I had kicked in her door and pushed her down the stairs of her apartment the previous week. She had taken out a restraining order against me, and now I had a bench warrant out for my arrest. I was headed to jail. Milly and I were dumbfounded. And no one could get me out until the judge saw me the following day.

The police were friendly and polite. They knew I had been railroaded, so they put me in the most comfortable cell they had and fed me food from McDonald's. The next morning, they fed me again and put me and others in a van to take us to court.

They assigned an attorney to stand beside me in court while I pled "not guilty." The judge released me on my own recognizance and set a trial date for two weeks later. Apparently, after Thanksgiving, Carrol had gone to family court and made up the lie. She convinced a neighbor to testify as a witness, and the judge believed them.

When my case was presented, the prosecuting attorney told the judge he would like to dismiss the case. The neighbor confessed the assault never happened. The case was dropped. However, the restraining order remained. I would have to return later to address that issue.

I had some serious thinking to do. On the one hand, I wanted to be with Candice. On the other hand, Carrol could seemingly make up any lie and have me jailed. I did not want my family, Milly, or Xavier to get hurt. I decided to leave the restraining order in place for three years. Candice was five years old, and I could see her again at eight.

Over the next few months, Milly and John became what I believed to be just good friends. Milly worked the third shift like John, and they spent a lot of time hanging out together. John had a small beach house near Horseneck Beach in Massachusetts. Milly said he could use some help cleaning the house. So, Milly and I drove to his house, which was a mess. But by the time we left, I felt as if I had helped a friend.

One day, my father asked, "Don't you think Milly and John are spending too much time together without you?"

"Nah. Milly would never cheat on me. I trust her. He doesn't stand a chance," I said.

This was my second warning.

A month later, Milly approached me and said, "Don't let me do anything stupid that I can't take back."

I was confused and asked her what she was talking about. She told me to forget about it—my third warning.

Over the next few months, Milly worked the third shift, and I worked first. We rarely saw each other. Before long, we had severe problems in our relationship and felt weird around each other. A few arguments popped up, and suddenly, the idea of splitting up and my moving out became a real option. Instead, we moved into another house on Clinton Street in Johnston, Rhode Island.

On the one hand, my new life was filled with promise. I had a wife whom I loved dearly and who adored me. We developed what seemed to be an unbreakable bond. On the other hand, my old life still tormented me, and it was almost impossible to bring the one good part of that life, my beautiful daughter Candice, into my new life. I had to leave my daughter and pray she would be okay.

Sometimes, forgiving ourselves is difficult. We either choose or feel forced to choose and then have second thoughts. We think of the "what if's" or the "if only's." The worst is "maybe I should have."

We can't possibly see life's whole picture. We never have all the truth or information. We only know what's in front of us at any given moment. We make judgments based on what we know from the past and do our best. Only God is all-knowing. That is why we need to pray for guidance. In the meantime, we must check our hearts, motives, and good intentions. Then, we must forgive ourselves when we fall short.

# Marriage

*"Get rid of all bitterness, rage and anger, brawling and slander, along with every form of malice. Be kind and compassionate to one another, forgiving each other, just as in Christ God forgave you."*

Ephesians 4:31-32

Unresolved anger will consume us. It will become a part of us and eat at us. Unfortunately, we may never know this is happening or how it affects us until it's too late.

Only God can take it from us. But as long as we feel we don't need a relationship with God, we will be left with destructive anger. Satan can tell when someone is full of rage. He hears us, sees us, and senses the anger in us. Then he whispers in our ears. Because we have no relationship with God, we can only rely on our own sinful understanding.

Milly and I had lived on Clinton Street for a few months when Milly became pregnant with our first baby. I was overjoyed. The child I had longed for with the woman I loved was finally on the way.

The pregnancy was uneventful. Milly continued to work at the prison but was moved to the day shift and promoted to lieutenant, where she oversaw inmates and their visitors. John was still around, but he and Milly did not see each other as much once she changed shifts. I felt he might have contributed to Milly and me almost breaking up, and I asked Milly not to see him anymore. I thought he interfered with our relationship. She agreed.

I was in the delivery room when our little Sammy girl arrived on February 22. We named her Samantha after my grandfather, Samuel—Samantha Arelis Major with the initials SAM. I instantly fell in love with our new addition.

Even after Milly agreed not to see John, I found evidence he was still around. She let him babysit Samantha from time to time, even after I told her several times I wanted him out of our lives. The more she saw him, the bigger our problems would be.

After almost a year, Milly told me the truth. John had threatened her. If she didn't let him see Samantha, he would tell me they had had an affair. John thought he was Samantha's father and wanted a DNA test to prove it.

Nothing had ever hurt me so much, but I stayed calm. I could see the hurt on Milly's face as she told me the truth. I agreed to the DNA test, hoping to prove John was not the father.

I don't remember all the details of this situation, but I remember telling Milly I was not leaving. I loved her and wanted no one else. I think I went numb when I first learned about the affair.

When the test came back, it showed that Samantha was, indeed, John's biological child. This didn't matter to me. I was madly in love with Milly and Samantha.

Our apartment was too small, so we contacted a real estate agent and a lender. I discovered we could afford a mortgage and buy our own home. This was important because I wanted Xavier and Samantha to have a place where they could put down roots and call home.

We found a home on Kensington Street in Smithfield, Rhode Island, with three bedrooms and a large living and dining room. Since it was a split-level house, we had living space on the lower level also, which meant we could bring my father back to live with us. So, we were all set up for the long haul.

After a few months, Milly approached me one day before she left for work and said she wanted to leave. I was devastated, and I didn't understand why. When I told my mother, she told me to talk with Milly to find out.

When Milly got home, I asked her about the reason she wanted to leave. She explained that it was my constantly bringing up her affair with John. If I was going to forgive her, I needed to stop resurrecting the affair. She would not live with me if I couldn't forgive her and let it go. She was right. On the occasions when I brought it up, I was mean, vulgar, harsh, and extremely hurtful to her.

Something in my mind shifted the blame. So, I made it all John's fault. Blaming him was easier than blaming Milly. And getting angry at him was also easier.

My mind took off with this anger. Milly had to see John to drop off Samantha for visitation. They met at a donut shop near the prison where they worked. Anytime I was to accompany Milly to the drop-off or pick-up time, she had to leave me at a nearby store. With all the rage and anger that had built up inside of me, I would have fought with John and probably caused him great harm.

As I waited, I angrily paced, looking in their direction and wondering whether I was a fool for staying in this situation.

Sometimes, I thought about going where they were to see what they were doing, but I never did. I feared what I might do if Milly was unfaithful to me again.

This cycle continued for years. Over time, my suspicions about Milly and John lessened as Milly proved her loyalty and love to me. I don't think she even knew the extent of what I went through. Eventually, John found another woman, who accompanied him on the pickups. This also helped to quench any suspicions.

My obsession with revenge was out of control for years. I would think about all the ways I could harm him. But of course, most, if not all, of these obsessive thoughts came when I was alone, and I didn't share them with anyone. As time went on, I became less obsessed with John.

Meanwhile, Milly and I were doing well. We kept the fact that John was Samantha's father from most everyone, telling only on a "need-to-know" basis. My father didn't even know. Then, on Father's Day 2000, my beautiful Kimberly was born. We named her Kimberly Irene (after my grandmother Irene) Major—initials KIM.

My work at Teknor Apex went well, but I started smoking cigarettes again when I learned that John was Samantha's father. By now, I had given up the habit for nearly five years. I think this was the first step in my rebellion against our marriage. After that, when Milly asked me why I smelled like smoke, I would lie and tell her I worked near a co-worker who smoked. For fear of losing Milly, I just lied and denied it.

My smoking led to a lot of smoke breaks at work. The designated smoking area was a picnic table outside. People around the table talked, had discussions, and got to know one another. Over time, I became close with a woman named Rose, a fondness I knew would upset Milly.

Although I played the part of a good husband, Milly and I slowly drifted apart. Milly's job changed, putting her on the second shift. She made more money but had less time with the kids and me.

Before I knew it, I was feeding the kids, taking them to daycare and picking them up, putting them to bed, being there for Xavier, and seeing Milly for about one hour per day. I felt like a single parent raising three kids. The only bright spot was that the restraining order against my seeing Candice was finally set to expire.

At the same time, the housing market went crazy, and we found ourselves sitting on a ton of equity. So, we decided to invest in some land, which we found in Maine. We bought thirteen acres in Lovell, Maine, and then purchased a thirty-two-foot camper to leave there, so we could have a place to stay. Soon after, on a whim because my old truck was breaking down, Milly bought me a new Chevrolet Silverado pickup.

One time, during a weekend in Maine, while we all sat around the campfire, I looked up at the night sky and said a prayer, thanking God for this beautiful place. Milly and I never prayed, so this seemed unusual but appropriate.

Later, Milly's mom decided she wanted to move to South Carolina, so we bought her a home there. In addition to a new truck, new car, land in Maine, and a camper, we now had a second home and supported Milly's mother. Still, something was missing.

Our marital problems mounted. Without any real guidance in truth, we both believed intimacy in the bedroom gaged our marital health. Since we shared little to no intimacy, we both felt our relationship was falling apart.

Through my friend Rose at work, I met Donna. Donna was pretty, and I also learned she was facing difficulties in her marriage. Before long, we were meeting in the early mornings and at lunchtime. On at least one occasion, I was unfaithful to Milly.

My time with Donna didn't last but a month or so. It became too much work to figure out when we could meet, and the adrenaline rush of a new relationship seemed to wear off. We both knew our relationship would never go anywhere, so without any complications, it just faded away.

I often felt I had forgiven Milly for cheating on me. I was wrong. I hadn't forgiven anyone. I even blamed myself for not seeing the signs and being so prideful about our relationship.

Blame-shifting is something we all do. It somehow makes dealing with our hurt easier than facing the truth. However, it isn't easier. Blame shifting redirects the pain and becomes even more destructive because it spreads.

In my case, the blame-shifting spread everywhere. My relationship with Milly stopped; my respect for my marriage stopped; and I became bitter and lonely. I also became a liar and eventually an adulterer. But the most destructive spread was giving John a double dose of anger, hatred, and disdain.

This is what happens when we don't forgive. The offense against us takes over. We feel as though we're letting someone get away with something if we forgive them, but we are actually entrapping ourselves.

I don't think we can forgive unless we know what it's like to be forgiven. That's why turning to God is so important. He has forgiven us for so much more. God leads by example.

# Forgiveness

*"I sought the LORD, and he answered me;*
*he delivered me from all my fears."*

Psalm 34:4

At my lowest, when I had nothing left and all seemed lost, I turned to the only One I thought might be able to do something. Only when we give up on our abilities will Jesus step in, but we must ask. If we don't ask, we are still trying to maintain control and haven't reached the bottom yet. Jesus is at the bottom.

This is why it's so important for believers to share the Good News of Jesus Christ. We must tell everyone about Him, so they know Whom to ask for help when they hit bottom. And when God delivers, He does so in a big way, so we know it was Him.

I didn't have any more affairs after Donna. But my flirting with other women didn't stop.

For nearly five years, Milly and I enjoyed our time in Maine. Our visits were the highlight of our year. I had asked my dad several times to come and visit, but he always had an excuse. Finally, he accepted, as did my friend, Stanley, and I was so excited to have a weekend with them at the camper in Maine.

Sadly, when we reached the campsite, we discovered someone had broken into the trailer and the shed I had built to store all my belongings. The thief stole all my camping equipment, including an expensive Honda generator that I used to power the trailer. I felt betrayed by Maine.

After that, I never thought of Maine in the same way again. So, when I finally left, I never went back. I left everything the way it was after the break-in. No clean-up. No collecting anything that was left. Just goodbye.

A friend of mine, Tommy, had become the plant manager at one of Teknor Apex's other manufacturing plants in Fountain Inn, South Carolina, only a few miles from the house we had purchased for Nelly. Tommy called to offer me a job there. Milly wanted me to apply. She loved the idea of being close to her mom again. I thought getting the job was a long shot for me, but after just a few weeks, I was chosen for the job.

Milly and the girls were excited about moving. Nelly was happy that she wouldn't be alone in South Carolina anymore. Xavier had graduated high school and enrolled in the 115th Military Police Company in the Army National Guard, the same unit I served in during Desert Storm. Candice was back living with her mother.

My father didn't like our move. When I had initially asked him to move in with us, I promised him I would never leave him and that I would always care for him. Unfortunately, my moving to South Carolina meant he would need to move in with his girlfriend, Claire, something he didn't want to do. It hurt to break my promise to him.

When I learned I was going to the "Bible Belt," I thought I might look for a church—something that wasn't Catholic because the

Catholic religion didn't do anything for me. Kevin, a co-worker, mentioned that he was Christian, and occasionally, I popped into his office to ask him questions about his faith. I asked about his church, and he would give me an answer that prompted more questions. One day, he asked if I wanted to visit his church—Brookwood Church in Simpsonville. I accepted the offer.

I did all this alone because Milly was still in Rhode Island, wrapping up things. When I got to Kevin's church, I was amazed at the size and confused because it didn't look like a church. It looked more like an institution.

Nervously, I went inside and found Kevin in a huge lobby. He showed me around. I saw complimentary coffee and donuts, classrooms, large rooms with little stages set up for music, bookstores, and a café. I remember asking him how much it cost to attend. He told me it was free.

Then Kevin showed me the main sanctuary. It looked like a movie theater with enough seating for twenty-five hundred people. Four large-screen TVs faced the audience, and production cameras were mixed in with the seating.

My eyes grew as wide as dinner plates, trying to take all this in. Kevin asked where I wanted to sit. I remembered my mother telling me to beware of cults when I came down South, so I told Kevin I wanted to sit in the back with my back against the wall and up high where I could see everyone.

Dark shadows of people arrived on the stage, taking their instruments. On the big screens, a clock ticked down two minutes until starting time. Then, the band started playing, and it was loud, like rock music. They sang about Jesus, and, almost on cue, everyone stood. Many raised their hands. I had never seen anything like this and couldn't believe this was church.

After a few songs, the band stopped, and someone said a nice prayer as the band left the stage. Then, a guy in jeans, sneakers, and a button-down shirt approached the microphone at center stage. He didn't look anything like what I expected a preacher to look like. I was accustomed to seeing robes like in the Catholic church.

He talked and talked, but I was so distracted by the visual stuff that I didn't hear a word he said—except for one thing: "You can't go to Heaven with hatred in your heart." I remember thinking, *Well, I guess I'm never going to Heaven because I hate John.*

On the way home, something extraordinary happened. I discovered I liked the church and wanted to return. So, I called Milly and told her about my experience. As I did, I cried. I didn't understand half of what had happened, but I choked up, anyway. I was confused about the crying. Why would something as mundane as finding a church cause such an emotional response in me?

I went to Brookwood Church a few more times by myself before Milly and the girls moved from Rhode Island. When they finally arrived, I took the whole family to church. I learned Brookwood had a special place for the kids to play and learn about Jesus while Milly and I sat in the sanctuary and enjoyed the service.

We enjoyed church for a while, but even that started to get more complicated as Milly and I continued to drift apart. We thought our move to South Carolina might give our relationship a boost. I made more money; Milly could find a good job; we were closer to her mom; we had found a new church. But none of that seemed to matter. And almost none of it worked out the way we planned.

I earned more money, but my relationship with my boss became more difficult. And the house we bought for her mother was not large enough for all of us. So, after Milly found a job, we moved out of my mother-in-law's house and into an apartment. Also, around this time, my father was diagnosed with lung cancer.

My time at home became more and more uncomfortable. I spent a lot of time on my laptop playing *Call of Duty*. If I wasn't doing that, I was in a chat room flirting with someone and hiding it from Milly. Milly spent time on her computer playing *Lineage*, a virtual reality game.

These two hobbies kept us from dealing with our problems. We had no idea how we got here or how to fix it, so we just went into our separate worlds to pass the time. We never openly fought with each other, so the girls never suspected anything was wrong.

On Wednesday, March 11, 2009, Milly asked me to join her for lunch at our favorite Chinese restaurant. I loved the food there, so I was excited. After the waiter took our order, Milly put her hands on the table, looked me in the eye, and asked, "Have you ever cheated on me?"

My heart sank and began pounding so loudly, I thought everyone could hear it. I did my best to maintain my composure and said, "No, honey, of course not."

She said, "You're a liar," then got up and left.

I was speechless and baffled. I headed back to work, not knowing what else to do. Before I got there, I called her and mumbled something about it being a long time ago when I was upset about her and John. She hung up on me. I realized I needed to see her immediately, so I turned around and headed home.

Nothing had prepared me for what happened next. Milly had always been so strong, but now, she was crying uncontrollably. I had never seen her so hurt. She told me she thought I was different. I had crushed her image of me. I was not the man she thought I was. I saw the pain I had caused her, and it disturbed me.

I fell to my knees. I was so mad at myself that I punched the concrete floor and broke my hand. She sat on the edge of our bed, opened my laptop, and tried to show me the flirtatious conversations I'd had in the chat rooms.

I didn't need to see those. I knew what I had done. I began punching and smashing the computer with my fists; then I went to the closet and grabbed a bag to pack some clothes. I was so ashamed of myself.

"Where are you going?" she asked.

"I am going to Rhode Island. I'm sure you don't want me around anymore."

As I drove, I remembered how things were during my divorce from Carrol. I remembered that I had experienced suicidal thoughts, and I didn't even like Carrol. The depression level was so great that the thoughts automatically popped into my mind. Because I loved Milly so much and I was the one who had caused her so much hurt and pain, I already feared what thoughts might pop into my mind.

Rather than go directly to Rhode Island, I decided to get some help first. So, I went to a gas station and asked the attendant if she knew of a mental hospital nearby. She gave me directions, but as I started down the road, Milly called and told me to come home. I didn't want to, but after several calls, she convinced me.

When I got home, Milly had calmed down quite a bit. I was so ashamed, I could hardly look at her. But she comforted me, then took me to a medical clinic to care for my hand. To have Milly care for me, even after I had hurt her so much, encouraged me.

On Thursday, March 12, 2009, I spent the entire day at my desk at work, repeating, "God, please give me her pain. I need a miracle." Time seemed to have stopped. My only thought throughout the day was, "God, please give me her pain. I need a miracle."

All I wanted was for Milly to somehow not hurt anymore—even if it meant I took her hurt—and a miracle that would somehow save my marriage. I believed it was over. God was the only One Who could make these two things happen. I just kept repeating, "God, please give me her pain. I need a miracle."

My office cubical was tucked in the back, so no one saw me. The idea of eating lunch repulsed me. I felt as if I didn't deserve the pleasure of eating. I had nowhere to turn, so I turned to God. Even if my marriage ended, God could give me the pain so Milly wouldn't have to suffer.

When I got home, Milly and I talked. I don't remember all of the conversation, but I remember one thing. I told her I always felt as if John was an evil monster who wanted to take my place. I believed he wanted Milly and wanted to be her husband. I hated him so much. I obsessed over the distain and loathing I had for him. This anger had consumed me for so long.

Milly looked at me and said, "He never wanted to take your place. He told me it would never work out between him and me and for me to stay with my husband."

I was shocked at hearing this.

"What? You never told me that."

"Yes, I did. You never listened."

I collapsed to the floor on my knees and cried uncontrollably. It was a deep, loud, and long sobbing that took my breath away. Then, the monster I had turned Joe into began to disappear. Something hard inside me cracked, and my hatred for John screamed out of me like steam from a pressure cooker. In its place, I felt forgiveness for John.

Right there, on the floor, in the middle of all this deep sobbing, the words I heard from the pastor at Brookwood Church rushed into my head: "You can't go to Heaven with hatred in your heart."

Suddenly, I heard another Voice. "Now, you can go to Heaven." Then the unimaginable happened. I began crying even harder for John, to the point I could hardly breathe. I was crying for my enemy. I had hated him so much, and he didn't even know. I had once loved that his daughter Samantha loved me more than him. Now all I felt was sorrow. I was suddenly so grateful that I had never carried out any of the acts of violence against him that I had often fantasized about.

Milly watched all this happen. She didn't understand what was going on with me. She just watched as I was curled up on the floor and sobbing. I didn't know how to explain it to her. I just told her that I believed I had forgiven John.

Friday, March 13, 2009, was a blur. The only clear thing I remember is that I decided to quit smoking. If I smoked and Milly asked me about it, I would have to lie, and I didn't plan to lie to her ever again.

On Saturday, March 14, 2009, Milly went to work, and the girls were playing at the neighbors. So, I was home alone. I thought about the crying and the events I had experienced on Thursday. Until that day, I had never cried much over anything.

At first, I tried to reason that maybe what happened was some kind of physical response to getting busted for cheating on Milly. I quickly dismissed that idea when I started putting the pieces together.

I remembered begging God to give me Milly's pain and to grant me a miracle. Then, I remembered that while I was bawling my eyes out, I had heard the pastor's words: "You can't go to Heaven with hate in your heart." John was the source of all my hate, and I miraculously found forgiveness for him. But then I heard another Voice. This Voice said, "You can now go to Heaven."

Why would the pastor's voice come into my head at such a profound time? Who said I could now go to Heaven? This was all about God. This was all about forgiveness! This was all about going to Heaven!

At that moment, I realized God was the One Who said I could go to Heaven. It was God Who had spoken to me. Again, I cried because I realized God took time out of His busy day to speak to me and that I mattered to God.

Then I had an amazing, miraculous epiphany: *God is real*. God had made all this happen. *He is real. Jesus is real. The Holy Spirit is real. They are all real.* I was awed, astonished, and amazed. And I was crying again; only this time, it was tears of great joy.

Was my recognition what it meant to be born again? It must be because nothing was the same anymore. I now knew God is real.

How could anything remain the same? All doubt had been removed, and God revealed Himself to me. This changed everything.

So why didn't everybody know this? This is like living in another dimension. It's like my whole life was in two dimension, and now I live in three dimensions. Why hadn't anyone ever told me? But they had. My mother had tried to tell me, but I had just rolled my eyes.

My next thought was about Milly. All I could think about now was Milly. I couldn't do this without her. We did everything together. Would she believe I had been born again? She worked in a prison. They were all born again once they got arrested and thrown into jail. She might think I was like those inmates.

My mind reeled from so much going on. I still needed to go about my day. I needed to get the laundry done. So, I went through the motions and drove to the laundry facility.

When I got there, I saw what appeared to be a bum doing his laundry. His hair was messed up; he had a beard and hadn't shaved; and he wore sweatpants and an old t-shirt. We made small talk, and he asked me what had happened to my hand. I told him that I punched the floor because I hurt someone I love. Then I finished loading the clothes and drove back to my apartment.

The guy was still there when I returned to move my clothes to the dryer. This time, he said he had a book for me that explained where God was during hard times. He said he had read it four times. I thought it must be a hard read. Then, he went out to his truck, and when he returned, he handed it to me. When I got home, I threw the book on the counter and didn't give it a second thought.

When I awoke the following day, I saw Milly sitting up in bed reading. I asked her what she was reading. She said she was reading the book I had left on the counter.

"This book is amazing," she said. "I've been reading it all night. I'm almost done."

"What's the name of the book, anyway?" I asked.

"*The Shack*. I've always known God was like this."

"What do you mean?" I asked.

"Every church I've been to made God seem as if He was angry and vindictive. This book describes God as loving and caring. I always felt God was that way. It's good to read a book that says God is loving."

We talked about the book, and I started reading it, too.

Within minutes, God was already working on Milly. He had brought a stranger into my world, who handed me a book meant for Milly. Milly saw God in a more meaningful and loving way. We didn't talk about the pain anymore. Instead, we talked about the book—and God.

My stubborn refusal to forgive almost led to the destruction of the one thing I valued most: my loving relationship with Milly. Holding on to anger and bitterness is fatal to any relationship. Holding on to this anger and bitterness is even more fatal than the offense itself because we carry the offense around. We go from being the *victim* to the *offender* of ourselves.

Many people make rash and dangerous choices because they refuse to give up their hurts. Instead, they make choices they otherwise would never make because the unforgiveness has changed their character. Letting go is difficult, especially when the offense is huge. We can't do it on our own. We need Someone more powerful than ourselves. We need God.

When I sat in my office and begged God to do something about my situation, I prayed the most earnest, heartfelt prayer I had ever prayed. I was desperate. I had nothing to give. I had nowhere else to turn. I was empty. I was also the one who had sinned against God, cheated on his wife, and lied for so long. But God saved me, anyway.

God did not stop there. I had begged Him to give me Milly's pain, but He took it instead. Without realizing it, I was sacrificing myself for my wife because I loved her that much. Jesus could relate.

I was so closed-minded about Joe that even when I heard the truth, I could not listen to it. But after begging God for a miracle, I finally heard the truth because God opened my mind. God's truth set me free by cracking open my hardened heart. All the hatred, bitterness, and disdain screamed out of me with every sobbing breath. I found complete forgiveness and compassion for the one person I hated.

God reminded me of what He had saved me from. He used my words and the words of a godly pastor to save my soul and reveal Himself. Then, He spoke to me and told me I could go to Heaven. God worked on Milly next, showing mercy and grace. With the help of the almighty God, we can know God is real. And so is forgiveness.

# Forgiveness Complete

Since Milly and I have become believers, we have talked more about God. We still have struggles with circumstances, but we now have victories over our circumstances. We give them both to God. We pray every day, say grace at mealtime, and attend church.

The most important thing that has changed in my life is reading the Bible. The Bible has taught me what love is and what it is not. I learn about God's character and how He has entered a relationship with me. He is now the Center of my marriage, and because He is the Center, I have never loved my wife more or felt more loved by her. Through Milly, God talks to me, loves me, holds me accountable, and corrects me. God has given me the most loving blessing I could receive in Milly.

I had forgiven John but needed to do more. While discussing forgiveness with Milly and my two girls at the dinner table, I decided to prove it—not to convince Milly but maybe more to confirm to her and me that the forgiveness was real. I asked Milly for her phone, and I called John. John answered, and I told him that God had changed my heart and that I forgave him for what happened in the past. All he could manage to say was thank you.

Four months later, John and his new family planned a trip to Disney. He asked if he could swing by on the way from Rhode

Island to Florida and pick up Samantha. I opened my home to John and his family to stay with us as they made their way to and from Disney so they wouldn't have to drive without rest or pay for a hotel. They accepted.

When I got John and his new wife by themselves, I shared my testimony with them. John heard everything—the good, the bad, and the ugly. I cried while telling him the part about crying for him and how forgiveness for him had overwhelmed me.

John was once my sworn enemy—or so I thought. But my real Enemy was God. When I finally lost the battle, Jesus saved me. As a result, the person I am today is not the same person I once was. The good things in me are the result of my choice to surrender myself to God's will. It began when I begged God for my wife's pain and a miracle to save my marriage. And God continues to change me.

Forgiveness is confirmed when we think of the person who offended us or the offense itself and feel nothing. But that isn't nearly as peaceful as being forgiven. My beautiful bride forgave me entirely for all my transgressions. She did not keep score or a record of my wrongs, and neither does God.

# Surrender

*Jesus replied, "Very truly I tell you, no one can see the kingdom of*
*God unless they are born again." "How can someone be born when*
*they are old?" Nicodemus asked. "Surely they cannot enter a second*
*time into their mother's womb to be born!" Jesus answered, "Very*
*truly I tell you, no one can enter the kingdom of God unless they*
*are born of water and the Spirit. Flesh gives birth to flesh, but*
*the Spirit gives birth to spirit. You should not be surprised at my*
*saying, "You must be born again."*

John 3:3-7

Jesus once said, "'Truly I tell you, people can be forgiven all their
sins and every slander they utter, but whoever blasphemes against
the Holy Spirit will never be forgiven; they are guilty of an eternal
sin'" (Mark 3:28-29).

I rolled my eyes when my mother said she was "born again." I
had no idea what she was talking about. I was so ignorant, but now,
I know. Being born of the flesh, of water, is obvious. It's our natural
birth. However, only those born again of the Spirit, our supernatural
birth, can understand it. Only believers will see God's Kingdom.

Through the new birth, we receive the Holy Spirit. Rejecting Him is the only unforgivable sin.

Growing up, I always thought going to Heaven was the default result of life, and you only went to Hell if you did something terrible. I think most people feel this way. Perhaps this idea came from my mother, who, as a Roman Catholic, believed people were saved as long as they were baptized as a baby.

We are all born separated from God and will remain that way unless we have a relationship with Him. The only way to do this is to accept the sacrifice for our sins that He provided through His Son, Jesus. Just as Jesus surrendered Himself for our sins, we must surrender ourselves for His forgiveness.

Regardless of what we grew up being taught, experiencing this new birth will most likely cause pain. But it is in this pain—where we have no place else to turn, where we have come to the end of ourselves—that we finally surrender to the One Who can make a way.

When God makes the way, His truth becomes ours. No one can take it away. No amount of argument, doubt, scientific reasoning, or temptation from Satan can remove God's truth.

The truth about God's existence is a game-changer; and with that truth comes a battle between good and evil, between God and Satan, between darkness and light, and between life and death. This battle has raged since the beginning. We engage in the war the moment we are conceived.

Believers are painfully aware of how personal this battle is. Before knowing Christ, we can be pretty comfortable in this broken world. So much so that we become our own god and will stop at nothing to keep anyone or anything from taking that godlike power away. We can only hear ourselves, not God.

Before believing in Christ, I was my own god. Even though I was taught about God when I was small, I never listened to or searched for Him. I thought I could handle life without Him.

I did not need the *real* God to save me until I had utterly failed. Then, after experiencing the pain of hurting the one I loved the most—a love more incredible than I had for myself—I surrendered it all, begged God for her pain, and then prayed for a miracle. At that time, I loved Milly as Jesus loves Milly. Jesus takes our pain, sacrifices Himself for us, and performs the miracle of resurrection—much as He resurrected my marriage.

What God did for me, He can do for you if you will come to the end of yourself and acknowledge your need for Him. It's not until we hit bottom and face the truth that there is no other way to overcome our situation except to turn to God that we can find Him.

Surrendering all we are to someone else goes against our nature—especially when the surrender is to Someone we can't see. But in that surrender is where we find God. God is supernatural and beyond our limited nature. Being born again is a supernatural, experiential event where we are made aware of God's existence and transformed into a new person.

My story is not unique. God has been changing people since the beginning of time. This is what He does. Jesus saves.

Forgiveness is renewing our minds and is associated with the new birth. Unfortunately, this world says we should not forgive. Many avenues promote a culture of vengeance, anger, and violence against anyone who wrongs us. These things and this mindset appeal to our nature. But God tells us to forgive and that vengeance belongs to Him. When we forgive as God forgives, forgiveness is real.

# Changed Character

God has continued to reveal Himself to me in many ways. Milly and I returned to the Chinese restaurant where I had previously lied to her. After all, it was our favorite one. She met me there for lunch, much like the last time. This time, however, we stayed for lunch and prayed over our food. We talked about God and our future.

When we finished, we held hands while walking to our cars. Before we separated, we gave each other a long hug and a kiss. At that moment, a stranger walked by and said, "Keep doing what you're doing."

I believed God was pleased with our love for each other and our efforts to put Him in the center. Imagine a triangle with you and your spouse at each end of the baseline. Then, imagine a line extending up from each of you to a center point above, forming a triangle. At the tip of the triangle is God.

At the base, you and your spouse cannot get any closer. Along that baseline is too much stuff that gets in the way: insecurity, doubts, hurts, emotional baggage, trust issues, and other people. On this baseline, we are only capable of a limited ability to love.

However, things change if we look at the line that leads to God and seek Him first. We can move closer to God by reading His Word and taking on His character. As we do, we inevitably overcome all that holds us back. As we look across the triangle, we see we can love each other more completely when God is at the center. With God living in our hearts through the indwelling Holy Spirit, we can see Him working in our lives.

Shortly after Milly and I believed, we experienced a lesson in God's provision. We were short on rent money. I knew things were tight, but Milly handled the finances, so she knew precisely how desperate our situation was.

I was at work when Milly called and asked me to take an early lunch. She had something for us to do. When I asked what was going on, she told me she had prayed about our financial situation while taking a shower. When she finished, she had an idea. Perhaps, we could sell something.

She went through her jewelry box and decided she would sell her emerald set—a necklace and matching earrings. She put them for sale on Craigslist for two hundred dollars, enough to cover the rent and buy dinner. Someone had contacted her immediately, and she wanted me to ride with her to meet the person.

I got permission from my boss and headed home. Along the way, I thought this might be a scam. Our meeting place was a local fast food restaurant but one on a seedy side of town, so I decided to take my handgun.

The gentleman came in with a small, metal box in his hand. My adrenaline increased as he sat down across from us. He opened his box and pulled out a scale, an eyepiece for looking closely at jewelry, and a calculator. My suspicions of some kind of set-up quickly vanished.

Milly first slid the box with the emerald set to him. He weighed it, examined it, pushed some buttons on his calculator, and said, "I'll give you one hundred dollars for it."

We were crushed. We needed two hundred. Milly slid the other box to him with some junk pieces she had brought. She hoped we could get at least another hundred. He took out each piece of junk and repeated the process. Again, he weighed and examined them, but he made separate piles this time. In all, we had about six pieces.

When he finished, he said, "I'll give you four hundred dollars for all of this."

"Including the emerald set?" I asked

"No. Four hundred just for this stuff," he said, pointing at the pieces of junk.

My wife's hand shot out like a rocket and grabbed the emerald set to keep, and we said, "Deal."

On the way home, as I praised God, He reminded me He was not concerned about how beautiful we looked, like the emerald set. He was more concerned about having a relationship with us, even if we looked like junk. He loves our wonderful mess. God is faithful and will always provide. We looked for two hundred dollars, but He gave us four hundred.

God has also shown me I can have deep conversations with Him. My pastor told me God communicates with us in various ways. I can remember the first time I had a lengthy conversation with God. I was driving on a business trip from Greenville, South Carolina, to Salisbury, North Carolina. I asked God a question about forgiveness. Much to my surprise, I received an answer immediately in my mind.

As I continued to ask more questions, the answers came almost before I could finish asking. At the end of the ride, I realized God and I had conversed for over an hour. I was disappointed when I reached my destination because the conversation had ended. We need to know God not only hears us when we are at our wit's end and have nothing left but that He also hears us anytime. We need to learn how to listen.

Many years have passed since I became a believer, and God has changed my character so much to align with His. My old self would never have approved of me now. I attend Bible studies and church and give much of my time and effort to helping others.

When Milly and I were saved and started regularly attending Brookwood Church, we learned of a class about improving communication with each other. We decided to join.

The instructor was a man who had been in a car accident some years earlier, leaving him a quadriplegic. He was among the happiest and most likable people I had ever met. I offered to help him with his exercises.

After offering to help many times, he finally accepted. In the beginning, he could only take about five to ten steps, which took nearly half an hour. Presently, he can walk four hundred feet in about two or three minutes.

God changes us. I have committed two nights every week for twelve years to helping someone. The old me was much too self-centered to uphold such a commitment.

Only because I have been born again am I the man Milly thought I was before she discovered I had cheated on her. I have since told her not to put her faith in me but in the One Who lives in me. And she can because she has the same Spirit in her.

I am by no means perfect. However, the difference is that I am keenly aware of my flaws, which matter now. Before I believed, I didn't care about lying, cheating, swearing, or other deviant behavior. It had no impact on me unless I got caught. Now, I measure the thoughts of those things and discard them before they happen because the Holy Spirit convicts me.

# Appendix

I didn't understand the concepts in this poem until more than thirty years later after first reading it. This is the poem I wrote to my mother while in the navy.

## The Cage

*There's two ways to live.*

*The way you choose*

*And the way God has to give.*

*You can accept His gift,*

*For you can be confident it's right.*

*Every time your spirit begins to lift in you,*

*You can feel His might.*

*The life you choose*

*Is with the flesh and a battle with Satan—*

*A battle the flesh is sure to lose,*

*A fight for which Satan is waiting.*

*For Satan is more powerful*

*Than any mortal man.*

*He will win any struggle.*

*Without the effort of the best, he can.*

*But we have one weapon*

*Stronger than the thickest, mightiest cord—*

*The only cord to hold and tie Satan,*

*We have the Lord.*

*We all realize and know*

*We all have weakness of the flesh*

*That Satan takes advantage of*

*To try and cage us in evil, steel mesh.*

*We are born halfway in the cage.*

*We are also halfway out.*

*Though the freedom of the Lord is questioned,*

*The reality of the cage we have no doubt.*

*We see people trapped all around us.*

*We see them every day.*

*They know there's only one escape.*

*Through Jesus is the only Way.*

*They try and try and try*

*To find some kind of happiness.*

*And when they fail, they cry,*

*All the while not knowing Who, how, when, or why.*

*Life seems like nothing but a struggle,*

*The earth nothing but a stage,*

*A fight that goes on forever*

*Between love, happiness, and the cage.*

*Love is something to be enjoyed.*

*Happiness is achieved through love.*

*The cage is always there.*

*Avoid it only through God above.*

*Avoiding the cage that Satan rules*

*Is not an easy task.*

*But God has given us a weapon,*

*Helpful only if you ask.*

*There is one thing you must know,*

*No matter how much wrong you do.*

*Jesus Christ our Savior*

*Has already provided forgiveness for you.*

*You must come to know Him*

*And claim your forgiveness and freedom*

*So that when you die, you'll be recognized*

*As chosen for God's Kingdom.*

*But while you're here on earth,*

*So long as you're filled with the Holy Spirit,*

*Where Satan's cage is concerned,*

*You won't even get near it.*

*You have the Holy Spirit in you.*

*The same as you're already forgiven,*

*Let God's Holy Spirit fill you,*

*For it's the best kind of living.*

The Holy Bible is God's Word, inspired by the Holy Spirt, Who lived in the heart of its authors. I believe this by faith and also because of this poem. At the time of its writing, I knew nothing about the concepts, nor would I ever use such language.

I believe the Holy Spirt came upon me for a brief time and for a specific purpose—to inspire me to write this poem. Although I sent it to my mother, I believe I was the Spirit's target audience. He merely gave the poem to my mother for safekeeping until I was ready for it.

The first time I read this poem after I became a believer, I was astounded. I cried with every word I read. I realized I needed to hear

God's truth from myself because I don't ever accept what people say as truth. I believe God used me to confirm my belief about Him.

# About the Author

Bruce Major is a veteran of the U.S. Navy and the U.S. Army. After believing in Christ, Bruce completed studies in Christian counseling, attended and hosted numerous Bible study groups, and experienced the work of God in his life in countless ways.

To learn more about Bruce, his testimony, or how to be born again, please visit his website at www.brucemajor.com or on Facebook at www.facebook.com/BruceMajorAuthor.

Ambassador International's mission is to magnify the Lord Jesus Christ and promote His Gospel through the written word.

We believe through the publication of Christian literature, Jesus Christ and His Word will be exalted, believers will be strengthened in their walk with Him, and the lost will be directed to Jesus Christ as the only way of salvation.

## For more information about
## AMBASSADOR INTERNATIONAL
## please visit:

*www.ambassador-international.com*
*@AmbassadorIntl*
*www.facebook.com/AmbassadorIntl*

*Thank you for reading this book!*

*You make it possible for us to fulfill our mission, and we are grateful for your partnership.*

*To help further our mission, please consider leaving us a review on your social media, favorite retailer's website, Goodreads or Bookbub, or our website.*

# More from Ambassador International

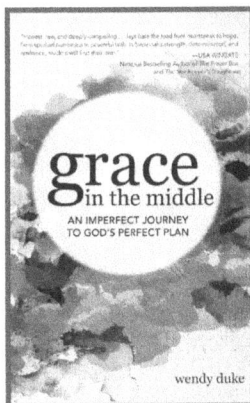

*Grace in the Middle* is a memoir recounting one young couple's struggle to hold on to an unraveling faith during the greatest crisis of their lives. Heartbreaking, triumphant, and funny in just the right places, this inspiring story is an authentic reflection on battling and overcoming physical illness and disability, resisting the dark doubts that plague us in the midst of tragedy, and trusting the faithfulness of God through the deep twists and turns of life.

Vanna Nguyen had escaped a war-ravaged Vietnam to life in America. Life seemed good and was finally settling down as Vanna planned a graduation party for her daughter Queena. But one phone call completely derailed those plans and sent Vanna and her daughters down a road they had never dreamed they would travel. The Bloomingdale Library Attack Survivor made a name for herself, but in a way no mother would ever want. Read about two women from the same family who fought against all odds to "make beauty from ashes."

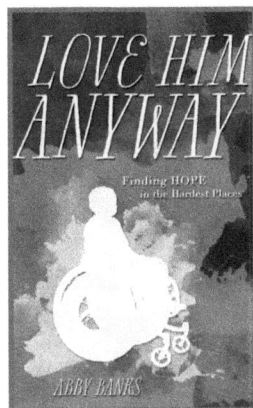

One night can change everything. Abby Banks put her healthy, happy infant son to sleep, but when she awoke the next morning, she felt as though she was living a nightmare. Her son, Wyatt, was paralyzed. In an instant, all her hopes and dreams for him were wiped away. As she struggled to come to grips with her son's devastating diagnosis and difficult rehabilitation, she found true hope in making a simple choice, a choice to love anyway—to love her son, the life she didn't plan, and the God of hope, Who is faithful even when the healing doesn't come.

www.ingramcontent.com/pod-product-compliance
Lightning Source LLC
Chambersburg PA
CBHW071053090426
42737CB00013B/2341